Salsa Brava
COCINA

Salsa Brava
COCINA

SMOKIN' SALSA AND OTHER INSPIRED RECIPES

BY JOHN CONLEY

PHOTOGRAPHY BY CHRISTOPHER MARCHETTI

Enjoy!
John Conley

LITTLE BEAR PUBLISHING

Composed in the United States of America
Printed in China

Production by Rudy Ramos
Designed by Rudy Ramos
Edited by Claudine J. Randazzo
Photography by Christopher Marchetti

First Impression 2009

09   10   11   12   1   2   3   4

ISBN-10: 0-615-28319-5
ISBN 13: 978-0-615-28319-7

The recipes contained in this book are to be followed exactly as written. The author is not responsible for your specific health or allergy requirements that may necessitate medical supervision, or for any adverse reactions to the recipes contained in this book.

For more information on Salsa Brava visit www.salsabravaflagstaff.com.

Dedicated to Genevieve Littlebear Conley, your eternal love, insight, and perseverance are inspiring, and to my daughter Sage Marie Littlebear Conley, the future is yours—go get it! May the world bring you happiness, warm kitchens to cook in, lush gardens that flourish, sunshine, and rain.

contents

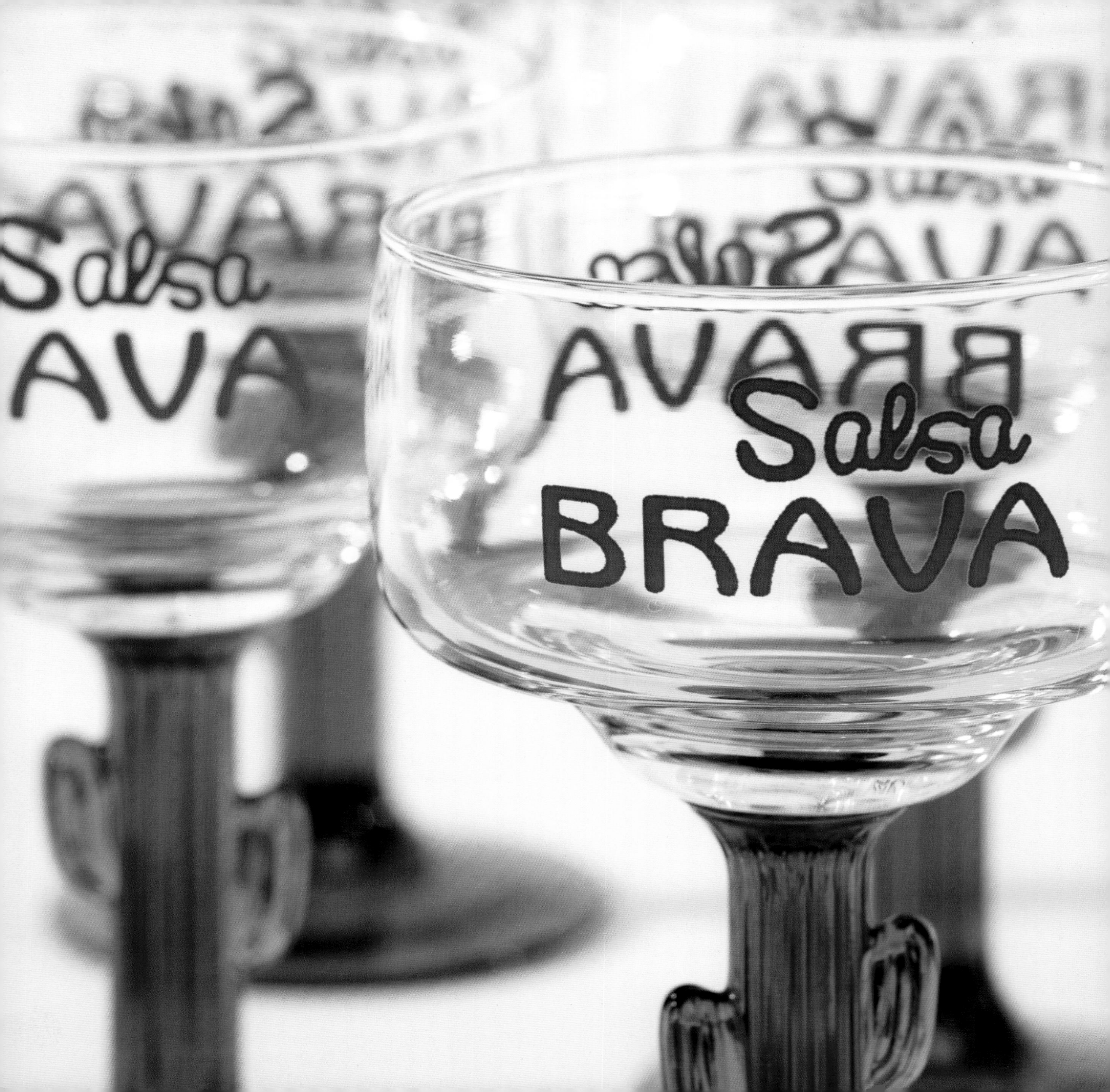
Salsa
BRAVA

introduction

I never expected to sit down long enough to gather my thoughts regarding my journey through this crazy culinary experience—let alone write a cookbook. I had originally set out to document a history of recipes that we've utilized throughout the years at Salsa Brava and make them available to our customers. I soon became aware that there was more to this than I had originally expected. I saw a theme in the history of what had first attracted me to cooking and ultimately led me down this beautiful road.

That theme, of course, is the food of Mexico, which is as diverse as its people, reflecting the influence of inhabitants past and present. The many layers of cultural attributes, starting from the old Indian civilizations to the introduction of the Spaniards, created not just food but an evolution of a food style that is really a culinary experience based on family, tradition, and necessity. In other words, here people do not just cook food; they live food.

These three things—family, tradition, necessity—plus community were the foundation of Mexican cooking, and they can still be found today in the country's many traditional celebrations. The family gatherings of *Día de los Muertos* (Day of the Dead), which occurs on November 1, has ancient Aztec and Mesoamerican roots. This day is set aside to remember and honor the lives of the deceased while celebrating the continuation of life. Halloween (October 31st) and All Souls' Day (November 2nd) are also locally important holidays. During this period, families celebrate the spirits of departed loved ones in various ways, including erecting *ofrendas* (small altars) in their houses, decorating tombs, and eating *calaveras* (skull-shaped candies) and sweet breads. It is a time for celebrating ancestors—with whom many believe they can communicate during these events—and embracing death as natural and inevitable rather than as something to be feared.

Many foods are indigenous to Mexico: corn, chiles, beans, tomatoes, and squash from the Aztec and Mayan Indians. The arrival of the Spaniards also brought beef, chicken, wine, pigs, olives, and rice. During the brief French rule, refined cooking techniques were introduced. Modern Mexican cuisine embodies an evolution that was shaped by all of these factors.

Today, Mexican cuisine is most often influenced by region. In the north, where wheat imported by the Spanish had great influence, more wheat dishes are prepared, as well as strongly spiced beef and pork.

To the south, many flavorful recipes are prepared that are entirely vegetarian or cooked with roasted chicken and even turkey. On the coast, of course, some of the finest seafood in the world is utilized to create another type of Mexican fare.

With such a great breadth of history and expression, it is easy to see why Mexican food is considered the most varied and unique in the world.

It is my hope that you, too, will experience the happiness and joy that has flowed so freely from so many sources—all surrounding the culinary traditions that I love. To cook is to express oneself, to feel, explore, and experience that which comes from within, that which came before, and that which lies ahead—to create something that has an existing basis, but to do it not by following rules but rather by following feelings. A recipe is only a thought, a road map with many detours. My hope is that you read between the lines and explore all the side roads.

The recipes that I share with you here have been served for more than twenty years at Salsa Brava. They are tried and true. They are constructed simply to allow for easy interpretation, duplication, and—hopefully—exploration. Take a leap, set out on a journey, grab the family, and go crazy in your kitchen.

A Su Salud—to your health.

John

John

about john

In the Beginning

Growing up in a family of nine has its advantages. Advantage one: a mom who is a great and creative cook—after all, she was feeding nine people everyday. I have fond memories of huge holiday gatherings and spending entire days in the kitchen watching my mom work her magic. Advantage two: I could, and would continually, get away with murder. Trying to oversee a monstrous family was difficult, and I reaped the benefits. I fell in love with cooking at an early age and realized that I could work many hours and not be missed; a check-in call was all that was required. I would leave early to work the breakfast shift and come home late after the dinner rush. Advantage three: in our busy house, if you didn't learn to cook, you went hungry. The kitchen was always open, and I never went hungry! Some of my first creations: fried bologna sandwiches stuffed with macaroni and cheese; hot dogs filled with Cheese Whiz (later this would be marketed nationally and someone—not me—would make millions).

We lived in Phoenix, Arizona, which allowed our family an abundance of Mexican food choices. I learned to appreciate, and then love and respect, Mexican food and Hispanic culture from an early age. El Bandito was the weekly stop for our family. My childhood memories are full of the sting of chile and the smell of freshly roasted Anaheims. Much like the Alaskans who stock their freezers with salmon, we stocked ours full of roasted green chiles.

Matzo Ball Soup—Chasing a Dream

It started twenty-nine years ago: I was an over-energetic, mischievous thirteen-year-old, washing dishes and busing tables at Katz Deli in Phoenix, Arizona. I had been working for Wanda and Howard Whelcher for about two months. One Saturday night, Leo the line cook had one too many, and come Sunday morning he didn't show up for work. I was there, however, and ready to work. It would be another busy Sunday morning, and this time it would be up to me to open the line.

During the previous two months, Leo had introduced me to the basics of cooking—flipping eggs, par-cooking bacon, blanching potatoes, and making potato pancake batter. It was time to put that new knowledge to use. Howard arrived at six-thirty in the morning; we opened at seven. "Where the !*#@ is Leo?" could be heard reverberating through the restaurant. The expletives just kept flying, and as Howard—the good man that he is—is also a boisterous man to say the least, this form of communication was from the belly, loud and intimidating. And he liked to throw things. Before entering the kitchen, he called Wanda for help. I could hear him getting angrier. The kitchen door slammed open, and I was about to make a run for it when Howard turned the corner, furious at expecting to have to set up the line, as he would have only fifteen minutes to do so. Except, the line was ready—eggs cracked, potatoes on the grill, and hot matzo ball soup simmering. He smiled, grumbled something, and walked out of the kitchen. And I was hooked!

Wanda arrived about a quarter after seven, and I had already managed to put out several tickets. By seven-thirty we were into it—fifteen tickets deep—with Wanda yelling egg orders to me while she assembled plates. It was fast and furious, and I loved it. The energy, the noise, the shouting—I felt at home.

I would go on to work and manage for Wanda and Howard through high school. I soaked up all that I could learn. Wanda taught me soups, stocks, sauces, desserts (to this day she still makes the best bread pudding), braised meats, and basic catering. Howard went on to teach me restaurant management via intimidation. It was a great balance—Wanda with a soft, motherly touch and Howard demonstrating the correct technique for throwing a knife through the kitchen window, a skill that would become an important one to be used at a later time.

A Slight Diversion

At the age of seventeen and much to my mom's chagrin, I decided it was time to leave home. I applied and was accepted to work for the United States Forest Service on the Heber Hotshots as a wild land firefighter in Heber, Arizona. The age requirement was eighteen, which I wasn't, but they thought I was. At the same time, I was accepted into the School of Hotel and Restaurant Management at Northern

Arizona University. My plan was to go to school in the fall and spring and fight fire during the summers and continue cooking during the off-season. One of the restaurants I would cook at was Salsa Brava.

It was a good balance, fighting fire during the summer months, attending NAU during the school year, and cooking. After one year in Heber, I applied for and was accepted into the rookie smokejumper class in Missoula, Montana. This was the experience of a lifetime; parachuting into fires had intrigued me for some time, and now I had the chance. This was a coveted position with nearly a thousand applicants per year. The rookie class consisted of twenty-five jumpers, and only twelve of us would make it. During this period I continued to cook wherever I could and as much as I could. I did most of the cooking and experimented with as many dishes as there were supplies for, so my fellow jumpers loved me. After five years with the Forest Service and multiple injuries, at the age of twenty-one, I decided to give up jumping and finish my degree. Upon returning to Flagstaff, I also returned to my job at Salsa Brava, only to learn that the owner Regina was going to sell the restaurant. It was underperforming, and she wanted to go into real estate. There was no doubt in my mind that I wanted to buy Salsa Brava. I had managed to save money from working as a smoke jumper, and I proposed to Regina the idea of selling the restaurant to me. She saw my enthusiasm and decided to take a big chance on a very young man. Before I knew it, we were hiring lawyers and drawing up agreements. It was my final year of college, but instead of finishing, I would drop out and, with a little down payment, a lot of luck, and an expensive note to pay off, have my first restaurant. I was scared and penniless. My family, school counselors, and many friends thought that I had gone crazy. At twenty-one years old, in the middle of my senior year at NAU, I was going to open my first restaurant.

A New Beginning

Originally, Salsa Brava offered strictly counter service with a limited menu. The restaurant could accommodate about twenty people. It was time for a change. My plan was to close down, convert the restaurant to full-service, and completely redo the menu by adding new items that many people had never experienced, for example, pollo con mole, bistec ranchero, adobos, barbecoas, and fish and shrimp tacos.

Through many travels to Mexico, I had acquired a love of the food as well as the people. Mexico intrigued me, and I spent as much time south of the border as possible, camping from beach to beach, and through the years managing to travel the entire western coast and much of the interior. The northern state of Sonora was always my jumping-off point. Sonora is rich with seafood from the Sea of Cortez, fresh range-fed Sonoran beef, an abundance of produce, and a multitude of chiles. It was a culinary smorgasbord. I knew that I had found my niche; now I just needed to make it into a restaurant.

Besides focusing on renovations and creating a new menu, I had managed to acquire an assistant cook. However, the "help wanted" sign advertising a need for food servers hung in the front door for nearly a week, but there were no bites. I was standing behind the cooking line attending to some last minute details when I heard the front door open. In walked this tall blonde inquiring about the sign. I had no experience interviewing—in fact I had never done it before. After all, my qualifications fell in the realm of the kitchen. My only focus was to find help. This woman, Genevieve, said that she had experience in food service. All I could see was this beautiful woman standing before me. "You're hired," I said, "if you can start right now." I had no idea whom I had just hired. In four years' time, Genevieve would become the love of my life, my best friend, my wife, and the mother of our children.

After a month of renovation, research, development, and training, opening day for Salsa Brava came and went without much fanfare. Customer counts were fair. Word started getting out, and soon we began to grow, allowing me to hire more staff and additional kitchen help. Introducing a new brand of Mexican food to the Flagstaff market proved to be working. It was hard work, but I loved it. That first year I did not take one day off, and to my amazement, by the end of the year I had turned a small profit. Despite the success, the first year at Salsa Brava was hard. Actually, it was almost impossible. I had a vision for the food and was able to execute that vision onto the plate. Business was good, but the front of the house was lacking. I had good people but found it difficult to balance the kitchen and the dining room, and as a result there was much confusion and no overall vision. I would try to micro-manage the dining room and still try to focus on the food. There was a huge imbalance, and my kitchen rage and immaturity would spill out onto the dining room floor. Needless to say, I was not easy to work for, and it affected the relationships I had with the floor staff—especially Genevieve, who was now a lead server and a floor manager. To put it lightly, that first year Genevieve and I did not get along and did not like each other. The reality was that I was to blame; my management skills were deficient. I could execute my cooking skills and inspire my fellow coworkers in the kitchen, but I lacked the experience to motivate and lead on the floor. Thank God for the thick-skinned employees who stood with me during this tumultuous learning curve. I wish that I had a nickel for every mistake I made during this time. Thankfully I realized that I needed to let go of the floor and focus on the food, spend my energy were

it was best served, and allow the floor staff to do their jobs. Simply, I had to get out of the way.

It was not long before we outgrew the restaurant and needed to expand. The space next door became available, so I jumped at the opportunity. We expanded the dining room to accommodate eighty people, added a patio, bought a liquor license, built a cantina, and reconfigured the kitchen. More staff and managers were hired, and we had a grand re-opening. Then things really took off, and the rest is history…a history that eventually led me to say goodbye to that first location and make Salsa Brava's one and only home on historic Route 66.

During this incredible journey, Gen became my wife, and our family expanded to include three children—Sage, Adam, and Ivan. The journey also included ownership of many other restaurants. Eventually, when our family started to grow, the simultaneous management of many businesses became an unmanageable juggling act. Business was great, but I was miserable. I was no longer cooking, but instead trying to manage a staff of one-hundred plus employees and several management teams. I had lost sight of my passion and missed the days when I could just cook. Like many others, I learned the wise lesson of downsizing and sold everything except for Salsa Brava. I have since forgotten about perfection; I take a back seat when I can and allow the staff to do their thing. The view is much better, stress is lower, and on occasion I get to take a nap.

I love what Chris Bianca from Pizzeria Bianca in downtown Phoenix said: "No matter how important we think we are, we'll never be more important than the ingredient."

1. *Ivan ready to catch some fish in Mexico.*
2. *Sage landing a silver salmon in the Kenai River, Alaska*
3. *Adam enjoying a fun day of outdoor adventure.*

Here is a guy with the number-one rated pizzeria in America, he has one small restaurant that seats thirty people, a small staff, and a line out the door. He opens at five o'clock for dinner, and five minutes later there is a two-hour wait. He has appeared on *Martha Stewart* and *Oprah* and earned the 2003 James Beard Award as Best Chef in the Southwest. He has achieved rock-star status among his pizza peers and has drawn the praise of authors and critics. He also said, "I have not, nor do I aspire to make the best pizza. I create what I can with the greatest amount of love and let the chips fall."

Whoever says that more is better, come talk to me—I'll talk some sense into you. Less can be better; for me, family time is better time, and downsizing is really right sizing.

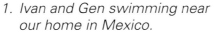

1. *Ivan and Gen swimming near our home in Mexico.*
2. *Ivan, heading back from a day's fishing.*
3. *Gen and John, sunset at the beach.*
4. *Sage and John, Playa Miramar, Mexico.*
5. *Adam, taking a break from body surfing.*

understanding chiles

I love chile peppers—always have and always will. At first it was *muy machismo*—ooh…watch how many I can eat! And then, a true relationship began with this fiery little beast, and hence, I've learned to use them in many ways. My wife Gen and I, along with our kids, still head for the border every chance we get and spend as much time as possible at our home in Playa Miramar, just south of Puerto Penasco on the upper end of the Sea of Cortez, also known as Rocky Point.

As one would imagine, here there are many taco shops, and we have tried them all. One of our favorites is Chino's. Chino has been making tacos for more than twenty years. When we started eating Chino's tacos, he was making them on the sidewalk out of a fifty-five gallon drum. He has since moved up to a taco cart, which is located near the fish market. The line is always ten deep, and everyone is willing to wait. The beef he uses is range-fed; his salsa is handmade hourly (his kids can be seen making Salsa de Molcajete, chopping like mad, throughout the day). My kids have grown up on this food and have experienced the sting of chiles many times. This is street food at its best—charbroiled carne asada piled high with fresh cabbage, lime juice, fresh roasted chiles, and an ice cold peñafiel for washing it all down.

Many people fear chiles, as they associate them only with a painful heat. The truth is that not all chiles are painfully hot, but all of them are packed full of flavor. So let's talk a little bit about chiles, their individual characteristics, and their "ratings," which will help in understanding the "hotness" factor.

Chile Ratings: Scoville Units

The Scoville scale was developed in 1912 by Wilbur Scoville. The method required puréeing chiles and mixing them with water sweetened with sugar. The scale measured the amount of sugar water required for a taster to no longer be able to detect the heat from the chile. If the amount of chile had to be diluted with 100,000 parts of sugar water to dilute the heat, then its heat was 100,000. Today, Scoville units are no longer measured by palates, but by machines.

The Scoville scale actually measures the amount of capsaicin in a chile. Capsaicinoid is the compound that creates the heat. Genes within the chile determine if it will be hot or not. The actual heat from a chile comes from the ribs on the inside, not the seeds as many people think. To help eliminate some of the heat when cooking with chiles, remove the ribs; by doing so, you will also remove the seeds, which can have a bitter taste. At Salsa Brava we do neither. We simply remove the stem and use the entire chile…we like the heat!

A chile's heat will vary due to how it is grown: the season, climate, and location. A stressed chile will have more heat. If you like to grow chiles and wish to make them hotter, try this method: after the chile plant has established itself and the stalk is secure, place pins or even nails through the stalk. This limits the water intake as well as stresses the veins in the stem. Chiles are hardy plants, and so this method should not kill them, but only make them work harder, thus developing a hotter chile.

CHILE TYPE	HEAT RATING (in Scoville heat units)
Habanero	200,000–300,000
Red Amazon	75,000
Pequín	75,000
Chiltepín	70,000–75,000
Tabasco	30,00–50,000
Cayenne	35,000
Arbol	25,000
Japone	25,000
Smoked Jalapeño (Chipotle)	10,000
Serrano	7,000–25,000
Puya	5,000
Guajillo	5,000
Jalapeño	3,500–4,500
Poblano	2,500–3,000
Pasilla	2,500
TAM Mild Jalepeño-1	1,000–1,500
Anaheim	1,000–1,400
New Mexican	1,000
Ancho	1,000
Bell & Pimiento	0

0–5,000: Mild 5,000–20,000: Medium 20,000–70,000: Hot 70,000–300,000: Extremely Hot

Habanero

I like to think of this as the mother of all chiles, not because it is the most widely used, but due to its versatility, allowing for many uses at Salsa Brava. One of our best salsas is the Blackened Pineapple Habanero Salsa. The habanero is native to the Caribbean, and the name actually means "Havana." Regionally it's most popular in Mexico's Yucatan. The habanero is also referred to as the Scotch Bonnet, and on the Scoville scale has a rating 1,000 times hotter than the jalapeño. Use gloves when handling these little devils. They also freeze well.

Poblano

Poblanos are mild, heart-shaped chiles that are large and have very thick walls, which make them great for stuffing. Chile rellenos are often made with poblanos. Poblanos are usually roasted and peeled before use, and when dried, they are called ancho or mulato chiles. The poblano rates between 1,000 and 2,000 Scoville units.

Chile de arbol

Chile de arbol is a narrow, curved chile that starts out green and matures to bright red. The arbol chile is very hot and related to the cayenne chile. Be careful during preparation. Arbol chiles are also the ones that are dried after turning red and used in many holiday wreaths. At Salsa Brava we roast hundreds of pounds of arbol chile; it adds a sweet, smoky flavor to many of our dishes. The chile de arbol rates between 15,000 and 30,000 Scoville units on the heat index.

Serrano

Serrano chiles have thin walls. They don't need to be steamed or peeled before using, making it the easiest chile to use for salsas. The serrano chile is green in color at first; it then ripens to red, brown, orange, or yellow. Serrano chiles don't dry well, since they are too meaty. The serrano is said to be about five times hotter than the jalapeño, rating between 8,000 and 22,000 Scoville units on the heat index.

Anaheim

These large, mild chiles are available in most local grocery stores. The green chile pepper may also be referred to as the Anaheim chile pepper, and it is related to the New Mexico green chile. They can be sliced, diced, peeled, and puréed. People who like to cook Mexican dishes find many uses for them. They are commonly roasted. This green chile pepper rates between 1,000 and 2,000 Scoville units on the heat index.

Ancho

Ancho is the name for a dried poblano pepper. Their average size and shape is two inches wide by four inches long with a pointed tip. They have a wrinkled skin, which is dark burgundy to almost black in color. Anchos yield a large amount of pulp relative to other chiles.

Chipotle

Chipotles are jalapeños that are dried over a warm smoke. The dried chiles are about two inches by one inch and have a dark brown color. They are usually purchased canned in a tomato sauce called adobo. The sauce is an excellent seasoning for beans or any other dish where a smoky spiciness is desired. Be sure to include equal amounts of the adobo in your recipes.

Guajillo

Guajillos vary in size, but an average one is about four inches by two inches with a blunt end. Their thick, brittle, and translucent skin is bright red, and they yield relatively little pulp.

Mulato

A mulato looks much like an ancho, but it is darker when held up to a light. They give food a medium-hot, non-sweet taste.

Pasilla

Pasillas are a long, narrow chile measuring about five inches by one inch. They have wrinkled skin and are very dark, almost black. Pasillas give food a hot and very complex flavor.

puerto penasco & the famous blue shrimp

In late 1949, fishing boats out of Guaymas began coming to the region known as Rocky Point where shrimp were abundant. Shrimp were easily caught by a simple net or a basket and consumed as a meal by the locals. That was until a man by the name of Victor Estrella took a sample of the region's blue shrimp to San Pedro, California. From then on, the Puerto Penasco shrimping business would never be the same. The sweet blue shrimp demanded the highest price on the market and was the most in demand. It was the beginning of Puerto Penasco's blue shrimp rush, which lasted until 1984.

It's All in the Name
More than one hundred years earlier, in 1826, the area received the name of Rocky Point from Lieutenant William Hale Hardy, retired officer of the Royal British Navy. He visited the area while in search for pearls and precious metals during his travels along the coast of Sonora and Baja, California. It was known on navigational charts by this name until 1936.

After being named by William Hale Hardy, Rocky Point continued to be a bleak desert spot visited only by occasional nomadic fishermen on their trips through the sea to the Gulf of Santa Clara or to San Felipe, Baja, California. Other visitors were brave Arizona sport fishermen who dared cross the great desert by road or trail to reach the sea.

Today, Puerto Penasco boasts a population of 65,000 and has become one of the pearls of Sonora. It is a destination for both tourists and sport fisherman and sees nearly one and a half million visitors each year.

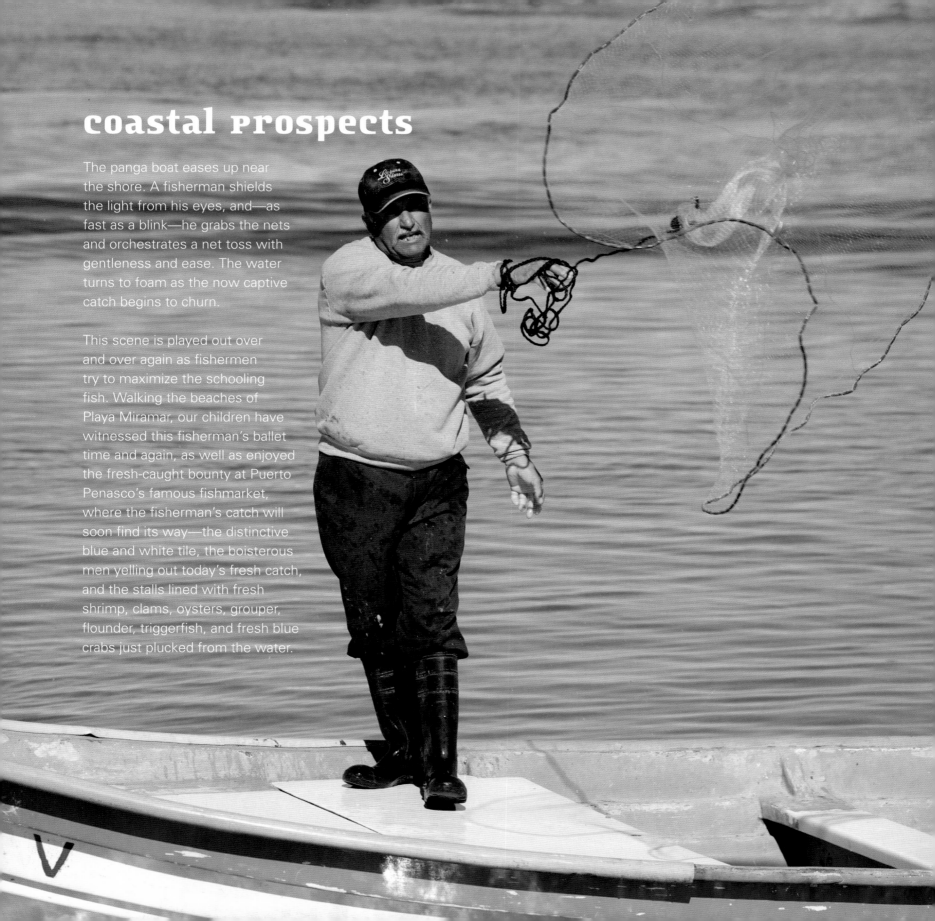

coastal prospects

The panga boat eases up near the shore. A fisherman shields the light from his eyes, and—as fast as a blink—he grabs the nets and orchestrates a net toss with gentleness and ease. The water turns to foam as the now captive catch begins to churn.

This scene is played out over and over again as fishermen try to maximize the schooling fish. Walking the beaches of Playa Miramar, our children have witnessed this fisherman's ballet time and again, as well as enjoyed the fresh-caught bounty at Puerto Penasco's famous fishmarket, where the fisherman's catch will soon find its way—the distinctive blue and white tile, the boisterous men yelling out today's fresh catch, and the stalls lined with fresh shrimp, clams, oysters, grouper, flounder, triggerfish, and fresh blue crabs just plucked from the water.

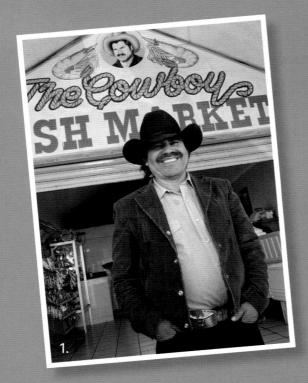

the people of puerto penasco

1. The cowboy fish salesman.
2. Selling sweet candies on the street.
3. Made-to-order tortillas.
4. Fresh pineapple bike cart.

1. Fresh Carne Asada.
2. Jumbo tortillas.
3. Fresh clams at the fishmarket, Puerto Penasco, Mexico.

1. Tacos al pastor.
2. Fresh oysters and asparagus.
3. Blue crabs.
4. Luca's famous pollo asado.

1. Old-timer, Puerto Penasco, Mexico.
2. Off for two weeks of shrimping.
3. View of Puerto Penasco's fishmarket.

salsa
our namesake

At Salsa Brava we use an average of 800 pounds of fresh tomatoes every week. Our salsas are handmade daily with chiles roasted on the open grill and fresh produce delivered daily from Flagstaff Farmers Market. Salsa has become the cornerstone to our success.

Salsa Brava became known for our salsa bar long before corporate America's Mexican chains exposed our little secret. Actually, it was no secret at all. Taquerias throughout Mexico have always supplied their little mesquite-fired taco stands with an abundance of toppings, such as cucumbers, radishes, marinated carrots, jalapeños, guacamole, and of course chile-infused salsas.

The origins of salsa sauce (a combination of chiles, tomatoes, and other spices) can be traced to the Aztecs, Mayans, and Incas. The Spaniards first encountered tomatoes after their conquest of Mexico between 1519–1521, which marked the beginning of the history of salsa sauce. Aztec lords combined tomatoes with chile peppers and ground squash seeds and consumed them mainly as a condiment served on turkey, venison, lobster, and fish. Today salsa can be found in almost every American home and now holds the distinction as America's most consumed condiment.

Blackened Tomato and Jalapeño salsa

This is by far the most requested salsa at Salsa Brava, and it is our version of Salsa de Molcajete. (Molcajete is a rock mortar used to crush fruits and roasted vegetables.) This salsa is one of the most common salsas in Mexico due to its simplicity and bold flavors. All that is needed is a hot fire or—for more practical home-cooking purposes—the oven broiler. Because most taco stands have a hot mesquite fire at the ready, this salsa is often prepared throughout the day. This is a rustic salsa and can be served chunky or flashed in the blender; you can determine the consistency you prefer. Perfect for the summertime, these ingredients can be thrown on the grill before the main entrée. The salsa is exceptional for dipping, huevos rancheros, nachos, beef, chicken, and pork dishes.
Makes 4 cups

Ingredients

3 medium tomatoes, about 2 pounds
4 fresh jalapeños, de-stemmed
½ medium sweet onion (preferably sweet Maui), sliced ¼-inch thick
5 garlic cloves, peeled

½ cup fresh cilantro, loosely packed, chopped
½ cup water or more as needed to get desired consistency
1 generous tablespoon salt (or to taste)

Preparation

1. *Heat the oven broiler to high. Lay the whole tomatoes, jalapeños, onions, and garlic on a broiler pan or baking sheet. Set the pan 4 inches below the broiler and broil for about 6 minutes, until the vegetables and chiles are darkly roasted and even blackened in spots (the tomato skins will split and curl in places). Using tongs, flip over the tomatoes, chiles, onions, and garlic and roast for another 6 minutes or so. The goal is to char all the vegetables but also to caramelize and cook them through to bring out the rich, smoky, sweet flavors. Cool for ten minutes and reserve all the juices.

2. Chop all the roasted vegetables and the cilantro to your desired consistency, mixing together in a bowl and adding water as needed. I recommend pulsing all the ingredients in a blender, adding the water slowly until arriving at the preferred thickness.

3. Taste and season with salt, remembering that this salsa will be hot. Use right away or cover and refrigerate for up to five days.

* Grilling option: Place all vegetables on the hot fire of a grill; roast them evenly, pulling off the chiles first, as they may cook a little faster than the other vegetables. When done roasting, remove from the grill and place in a non-reactive bowl and allow to cool for ten minutes, reserving all the juices.

roasted pineapple Habanero salsa

We tried to have this recipe duplicated by a major manufacturer, and the result was a disaster—not even close to our house-made salsa. It's hard to duplicate the same roasted flavor and texture provided by the slow roasting of the tomatoes and jalapeños and the sting of freshly blended habaneros. This salsa can be very hot, so adjust the heat by decreasing the habanero. Start with a small amount and increase accordingly. The habanero will be at its hottest as soon as you blend it then will mellow to a certain point and maintain this heat level. So when adjusting for heat, keep this in mind. The current recipe is designed to be a hot salsa; however, this is truly dictated by the individual chile: the time of year it was grown, the location where it was grown, and the amount of stress the chile was exposed to while growing.
Makes 6 cups

Ingredients

3 medium tomatoes, or 2 pound

4 jalapeños (1–1½ ounces), de-stemmed

¼ medium, sweet onion (preferably sweet Maui), sliced ¼-inch thick

½ cup water, or more to arrive at the desired consistency

½ cup cilantro, loosely packed, chopped

1 generous tablespoon salt (or to taste)

2 habaneros

1 can (27 ounce) pineapple tidbits (½-inch pieces with juice)

Preparation

1. Heat the oven broiler to high (or try the grilling option in the Blackened Tomato and Jalapeño Salsa recipe). Place the whole tomatoes, jalapeños, and onions on a broiler pan or baking sheet. Set the pan 4 inches below the broiler and broil for about 6 minutes, until darkly roasted and even blackened in spots on one side (the tomato skins will split and curl in places). Using tongs, flip over the tomatoes, chiles, and onions and roast the other side for another 6 minutes or so. The goal is to char all the vegetables but also to caramelize and cook them through to bring out the rich, smoky, sweet flavors. Cool for ten minutes, reserving all the juices.

2. Place half of the roasted vegetables, the habaneros, the can of pineapple and the juice, and half of the water and begin to pulse the mixture in a food processor or blender (we prefer this salsa to be evenly chopped but not puréed). Adjust the consistency by pulsing the salsa and adding the remaining roasted vegetables and the cilantro (pulse to the same consistency as your first batch).

3. Taste and season with salt and adjust the consistency with water. This salsa will thicken as it cools, so take this into account as you add water, remembering that it will be hotter at first then begin to mellow. Use right away or cover and refrigerate for up to 4 days.

roasted tomatillo chipotle salsa

This is a simple variation of Salsa Verde. The chipotle adds a little more heat and a distinctive smoky flavor. Chipotles are becoming widely used and are readily available at your local market—look for Chipotle in Adobo in small cans. Remember that a chipotle is a smoked jalapeño, and the adobo is the sauce that it creates when reconstituted. The canned products on the market are already reconstituted. Be sure to use the sauce (adobo) to add that distinctive smoky flavor.

Makes 3 cups

Ingredients
1½ pounds tomatillos
Juice of one lime
5 cloves garlic
5–10 chipotles in adobo (depending on preference
    for heat and smoked flavor)
1 medium onion, sliced
½ teaspoon sugar
½ cup cilantro
Salt to taste

Preparation
1. Remove husks from tomatillos and rinse well. Cut in half and place cut side down on a foil-lined baking sheet. Place under a broiler for about 5 to 7 minutes to lightly blacken the skin, or for better results roast whole tomatillos on an open grill.
2. Place tomatillos, lime juice, garlic, chipoltes, onions, cilantro, and sugar in a food processor (or blender) and pulse until all ingredients are finely chopped and well mixed. Season to taste with salt. Cool in refrigerator.

salsa de mariscos

Stop at any fish taco stand in Mexico, and the chances are good that you'll experience Salsa de Marisco.
The cucumber adds a crisp texture to the fish.
Makes 4 cups

Ingredients
3 to 4 large, ripe tomatoes, diced
1 large cucumber, peeled, seeds removed, and chopped
3 jalapeños, diced
1 medium, sweet onion (preferably sweet Maui), diced
1 cup chopped cilantro
1½ teaspoons salt (preferably sea salt or kosher salt), or to taste

Preparation
Combine all ingredients in a bowl and chill until serving.

tomatillo (tohm–ah–TEE–oh)

I wish that I had a nickel for every time someone called a tomatillo a green tomato, which it is not, has not been, and never will be. However, when de-husked and cleaned, it does resemble a not-quite-ripe tomato, hence the confusion. The flavor profile of a fresh tomatillo—tart and sometimes sweet—does not come close to that of a tomato. The tomatillo is actually a member of the gooseberry family, and it is very versatile and has many uses. Without tomatillos, there would be no salsa verde…no green sauce for chicken enchiladas, pork tamales, or green pumpkinseed mole sauce. Even sauces that appear to be made solely from red ingredients (red chiles) often get their characteristic perkiness from some well-blended tomatillos.

Raw, uncooked tomatillos add a fresh, tangy citrus-like flavor and are often used raw in Mexican table sauces. Finely dice or purée them for this use.

Blanching mellows the flavor. To blanch, bring a large pot of water to a boil. Add the whole tomatillos (husks removed and rinsed) and boil for about 5 minutes, until soft, then drain and crush or purée as directed in a sauce recipe.

When fire roasting, leaving the slightly blackened skins intact enriches a sauce with a smoky, woodsy flavor. They can be roasted under the broiler, with a propane torch, or over an open flame such as a grill or a gas burner. Make sure the heat is quite hot; otherwise, the tomatillos will turn mushy before becoming charred.

Dry roasting produces an earthy, nutty flavor. Place the tomatillos in a heavy skillet (preferably cast-iron). Turn the heat to low. Roast for about 20 to 30 minutes, turning occasionally, letting each side take on a rich, burnished golden color before turning.

Finally, tomatillos can be quite inconsistent in flavor, with some being intensely sour and others tasting mild and sweet. Some cooks use a pinch of sugar to balance the taste of very tart tomatillos. The recipes following are typical Mexican tomatillo recipes, but the lively flavors of this perky little fruit lend themselves well to much experimentation, from stir-fry to soups to salad dressings.

classic salsa verde

Tomatillos add a sweet, tart flavor to this classic salsa. This salsa is excellent with huevos rancheros.
Makes 3 cups

Ingredients
1½ pounds tomatillos
3 jalapeños, roasted
½ cup chopped white onion
½ cup cilantro leaves
Juice of one lime
¼ teaspoon sugar
Salt to taste
¼ cup water for blending

Preparation
1. Remove husks from tomatillos and rinse well. Cut in half and place cut side down on a foil-lined baking sheet along with jalapeños. Place under a broiler for about 5 to 7 minutes to lightly blacken the skin, or for better results, roast whole tomatillos on a open grill or on an dry cast iron skillet.
2. Place tomatillos, jalapeños, onions, cilantro, lime juice, and sugar in a food processor or blender and pulse until all ingredients are finely chopped and well mixed, adding the water to adjust the consistency. Season to taste with salt. Cool in the refrigerator.

Serve with chips or as a salsa accompaniment to Mexican dishes.

"If only we could apply in our daily lives the same love and kindness that Sage so willingly gives her tomato buds, the world would be a better place— one tomato at a time."

sage's salsa Fresca

My daughter Sage has a gift for gardening. With a little guidance, her garden has consistently supplied a bounty of fresh fruits and vegetables. And this year was no exception; she has supplied our household and our neighborhood with her bumper crop of tomatoes, which translates into a bumper crop of salsa at the Conley household. Her seven plants yielded hundreds of tomatoes. Not bad for an eleven-year-old!

It gives me much joy to see her take an interest in something that requires so much work and commitment. Somewhere she learned that if you touch each and every tomato flower and whisper sweet nothings to the flowering buds, her beloved plants would respond in kind. And respond they did. Never again will I question her gardening techniques. To see Sage sitting in the midst of her garden surrounded by tomatoes, melons, carrots, and peas—whispering sweet messages—is truly a sight.

And so, as a result of Sage's success, it was salsa time at the homestead, and Salsa Fresca became a staple. Salsa Fresca is simple and divine, especially when made with sun-drenched, vine-ripened tomatoes that have been whispered to by the sweet voice of an innocent child. Thanks, Sage!
Makes 4 cups

Ingredients
3 to 4 large ripe tomatoes (preferably from
    Sage's garden)
½ cup chopped cilantro
4 Anaheim green chiles, fire roasted, peeled,
    seeded, and diced (canned will suffice)
½ cup finely chopped red onion

1 teaspoon packed brown sugar
2 green onions, finely chopped
4–6 cloves garlic, finely minced
1 tablespoon salt, or to taste
2–4 fresh jalapeños, seeded and diced
Juice of 2 limes

Preparation
1. Combine all ingredients in a glass (or non-reactive) bowl. This salsa is always better the next day, but it can be served immediately.

2. Cover and refrigerate until ready to use. It will keep for up to a week in the refrigerator.

pico de Gallo

Let's dispel the rumors: What exactly is Pico de Gallo? No, it's not your tomato-based salsa with green chile, onions, jalapeños, cilantro, and the like. Yes, Pico de Gallo does translate into "beak of the rooster," but only because of the red chile used in the seasoning blend that resembles the color of the beak of the chicken. Contrary to popular belief, red Pico de Gallo is a fruit-based salsa. This is an awesome summertime salsa that will surprise and please your family and friends.
Makes 6 to 8 cups

Ingredients

1 apple, peeled, cored, and chopped
 into ½-inch pieces
½ of a cantaloupe, peeled, seeded, and cut into
 ½-inch pieces
1 cucumber, skin removed, sliced longways,
 seeds removed (cut julienne-style)
1 small jicama, peeled, sliced julienne-style
½ of a honeydew, peeled, seeded, and cut
 into ½-inch pieces

2 oranges, peeled (removing all the white rind),
 segments separated
Juice of 4 limes
2–3 tablespoons Pico de Gallo seasoning: use
 equal parts of fresh ground black pepper,
 kosher salt, garlic powder, ground hot red chile
 powder
(Other fruits, such as mango, kiwi, plum, or
 nectarine may be added.)

Preparation

1. Combine all fruit in a glass bowl, add seasoning
 and mix well.
2. Chill until ready to serve.

salsa chile de arbol

This is a fiery, hot salsa. Be careful when roasting the chile—make sure your kitchen exhaust vent works well. When making this salsa at home, I use the gas burner attached to my grill and roast the chile outside. The smoke from the roasted chile can cause irritation in the throat and eyes.

Makes about 5 cups

Ingredients

3 medium tomatoes, broiled on a baking sheet until charred (see roasting instructions page 2)

2 ounces canola oil

1⅓ cups arbol chiles, de-stemmed, roasted*

½ teaspoon ground black pepper

¾ pounds tomatillos (about 10), husks removed, rinsed, and broiled on a baking sheet until charred

½ bunch cilantro leaves, roughly chopped

½ white onion, roasted

3 garlic cloves, minced

1 cup water for blending

1 tablespoon salt, or to taste

Preparation

1. *Using a large sauté pan, warm the canola oil on high heat until the oil is smoking. Add all the arbol chiles, cooking while turning the chiles with a wooden spoon until they start to change color from bright red to brown (about 2 minutes). Remove from heat. Beware: this chile will smoke, so try to not get the smoke into your eyes or lungs.

2. Place all ingredients in a non-reactive pan and bring to a slow simmer until onions become soft.

3. Purée all ingredients in a food processor or a blender until you reach the desired consistency.

roasted corn salsa

Fire up the grill! Here's another great, summertime salsa that is quick and easy. Fresh corn roasted on the grill can't be matched for this roasted corn salsa.

Makes about 5 cups

Ingredients

Corn kernels from 5 ears roasted sweet yellow corn (see roasting methods below)

2 teaspoons olive oil

2 small Roma tomatoes, chopped

1 jalapeño, seeded and diced

3 tablespoons diced red pepper

2 garlic cloves, minced

3 tablespoons diced red pepper

2 tablespoons extra virgin olive oil

3 tablespoons chopped cilantro leaves

1 tablespoon fresh lime or lemon juice

½ teaspoon salt, or to taste (preferably sea salt or kosher salt)

$1/8$ teaspoon ground black pepper, or to taste

$1/8$ teaspoon ground cumin

Preparation

1. In a medium bowl, combine corn and remaining ingredients.
2. Cover and refrigerate until ready to serve. Bring to room temperature before using.

Roasting Corn—oven method:

1. Preheat oven to 400 degrees F.
2. Brush corn with olive oil and place on a baking sheet.
3. Roast 15 to 20 minutes until ears start to turn a light golden brown.

Roasting Corn—grill method:

1. Preheat grill to medium-high heat.
2. Place ears of corn directly on grill (olive oil is not needed).
3. Grill until corn turns a bright yellow with some of the kernels having turned black from the grilling process. (About 10 to 15 minutes on a hot grill.)

Black Bean and corn salsa salad

This is a unique and flavorful salsa-style salad. Adding black beans gives it substance, and the chiles give it color and spice.

Makes 10 servings

Ingredients

2 freshly cooked cups black beans, or 2 cans black beans (15 ounces each), rinsed and drained

$^1\!/_3$ cup olive oil

2 jalapeños, seeded and finely minced

1 small red or white sweet onion, finely chopped (¾ cup)

1 large ripe tomato, chopped

½ cup finely chopped cilantro

¼ cup fresh lime juice

2 garlic cloves, minced

½ teaspoon ground cumin

½ teaspoon ground coriander

1 small red bell pepper, seeded and chopped (¾ cup)

1 small orange bell pepper, seeded and chopped (¾ cup)

3 cups corn kernels (fresh corn boiled on the cob for 4 minutes and cooled is best)

Preparation

1. Drain and rinse the beans.
2. Mix all the ingredients, except the corn, together and set aside.
3. Add the corn kernels and fold them in gently. Some of the kernels will stick together; do not break them apart.
4. Chill for a few hours before serving.

tropical salsa

This salsa is great served with grilled sea bass, halibut, tilapia, or salmon.
Makes 3 to 4 cups

Ingredients
1 cup diced mango
1 cup diced fresh pineapple
$^2/_3$ cup diced cucumber
$^2/_3$ cup diced red pepper
3 tablespoons finely chopped green onions
1 teaspoon seeded and finely chopped jalapeño
2 tablespoons fresh lime juice
2 teaspoons extra virgin olive oil
¼ cup chopped cilantro
Salt to taste

Preparation
1. In a medium bowl, gently toss together mango, pineapple, cucumber, red pepper, green onion, jalapeño, lime juice, and olive oil.
2. Add cilantro and season to taste with salt.
3. Set aside until serving or refrigerate, covered, if making ahead of time.

seared pineapple salsa

This salsa works especially well with barbequed chicken, slow-roasted carnitas tacos, pork tenderloin, and pork adobado. It is also a great salsa for fish tacos.
Makes 4 cups

Ingredients
1 large, ripe pineapple, cut into ¼-inch pieces (3 to 3½ cups)
1 small, red bell pepper, diced
3 teaspoons puréed chipotle in adobo
1 tablespoon orange juice
2 tablespoons chopped cilantro
Juice of one lime
1 teaspoon brown sugar

Preparation
1. Using a nonstick sauté pan, dry-sear the pineapple over medium heat until the sugar in the pineapple begins to caramelize (10 to 15 minutes). Remove from heat and cool.
2. In a mixing bowl, combine all the other ingredients. Add the pineapple once it has cooled and mix well.
3. Adjust the flavor as needed with more chipotle purée, fruit juice, and salt.

"Cooking is like love. It should be entered into with abandon or not at all."
—Harriet Van Horne

mango salsa

This is one of the best fruit salsas. At Salsa Brava, we use this salsa to top our Blackened Salmon Fajitas and Salmon Tacos. We also serve it on the side with our Coconut Prawns.
Makes 4 cups

Ingredients
2 mangoes, peeled and diced (¼-inch pieces;
   3½ cups or 1¾ pounds)
¼ cup diced red pepper
¼ cup diced red onion
¼ cup chopped cilantro
Juice of three limes
2 jalapeños, cleaned and diced
⅛ teaspoon salt and pepper, or to taste

Preparation
Combine all ingredients and let stand at room temperature for 30 minutes.

"Go confidently in the direction of your dreams! Live the life you've imagined. As you simplify your life, the laws of the universe will be simpler."

—*Henry David Thoreau*

mercados

The pleasures of walking through a mercado are as much visual as salivary. The multi-color exhibitions of dried chiles and fresh fruits, hanging meats, grilling chicken, fresh fish caught that morning, and fresh fruit drinks can be a visual smorgasbord. From the huge mercados of Oaxaca and Guadalajara, to the small, street-side show of food and products in San Miguel de Allende, there is something for everybody. The mercado has preserved for its vendors and its shoppers some of Mexico's best traditions.

Appetizers

Antojitos—also known as "little whims" or *botanas*, which are usually eaten with drinks much like the Spanish tapas, not as a prelude to a meal, but rather served during time set aside for leisure, drinks, and conversation.

Appetizers, *antojitos*, *botanas*—whichever term is preferred—have always been a very fun and exciting part of our menu, a way to introduce new and exciting dishes that some patrons would not ordinarily try.

When traveling through Old Mexico, don't hesitate to try the street vendors' food. They dot nearly every street corner and most beach fronts and offer ceviche, shrimp cocktails, roasted corn with cotija cheese, fresh ripe mango on a stick, handmade sesame seed candies, or fresh cracked coconut with lime juice and red chile. These are truly appetizers; call them anticipatory snacks, a prelude of things to come, but know that these are healthy—not overly filling—and they leave room to enjoy the remaining culinary journey.

apple and Brie quesadillas with chipotle cream

This is a wonderful change from the ordinary quesadilla. The flavors of the brie along with the apple make for an extraordinary combination. We serve this as a special or at catered events in our quesadilla station. You can substitute pears for the apples, if you choose.
Serves 10

Ingredients
1 tablespoon vegetable oil
2 medium onions, sliced
$1/4$ cup balsamic vinegar
$1/8$ teaspoon sugar
$1/8$ teaspoon dried thyme
$1/8$ teaspoon dried rosemary, crushed
4 (10-inch) flour tortillas
2 medium tart apples, sliced
8 ounces Brie or Camembert cheese,
    rind removed and cut in quarters

Chipotle Cream:
$1/2$ cup sour cream
1 tablespoon of fresh lime or lemon juice
$1/2$ cup plain yogurt
2 tablespoons finely chopped canned chipoltes
    in adobo
Dash of salt
Combine all ingredients until well blended.

Preparation
1. Heat the oil in a skillet over medium heat and cook the onions, vinegar, sugar, thyme, and rosemary for 10 minutes or until onions are golden.
2. Spoon the mixture over half of each tortilla; top with apples and cheese and fold over.
3. Transfer to a griddle and cook over medium heat for 2–3 minutes on each side or until cheese is melted.
4. Transfer to a serving plate, top with chipotle cream, and serve.

coconut shrimp with marmalade dipping sauce

Serves 10 to 12

Ingredients
2 pounds jumbo shrimp
1 cup flour
1 cup cold beer or ice water
½ teaspoon sugar
½ teaspoon salt
2 tablespoons olive oil
1 egg
1 cup shredded coconut
1 cup corn or canola oil

Preparation
1. Peel, de-vein, and butterfly the shrimp, leaving the tails on. Rinse and pat dry.
2. In a mixing bowl, combine flour, beer, sugar, salt, olive oil, and egg. Set aside.
3. Place the chopped coconut on a plate.
4. Heat the oil in a deep fryer or deep skillet to medium-high heat.
5. Dip the shrimp, one at a time, in the beer batter and then roll in coconut. Carefully place the shrimp in the hot oil and cook until golden brown and crispy on each side.
6. Drain on paper towels. Serve with the dipping sauce.

Marmalade Dipping Sauce
Makes ¾ cup

Ingredients
½ cup orange marmalade
2 teaspoons stone-ground mustard (with whole-grain mustard seed)
1 teaspoon prepared horseradish
1 dash salt

Combine all ingredients in a small bowl and refrigerate for at least one hour before serving.

guacamole

This appetizer is synonymous with Mexican cooking. The variations for guacamole are as different as the variations for salsas. This is a great recipe that should be made as close to serving time as possible. At Salsa Brava we don't start the guacamole until a guest orders it, and even then it is prepared tableside to ensure freshness as well as allowing our guests to decide how they would like it prepared. Serve it with tortilla chips, nachos, tacos, burritos, omelets, quesadillas…the list goes on and on!
Serves 2 to 4

Ingredients

2-3 ripe avocados
½ red onion, minced (about ½ cup)
3 tablespoons cilantro leaves, finely chopped
1 tablespoon of fresh lime or lemon juice
½ teaspoon coarse kosher salt, or to taste
A dash of fresh ground black pepper
2 Anaheim chiles, fire roasted, seeded and chopped (canned are fine)
1–2 jalapeños, stems and seeds removed, minced
½ ripe tomato, chopped

Preparation

1. Cut avocados in half and remove the seed. Scoop out the avocado meat and place in a mixing bowl.
2. Mash the avocado using a fork. Add the chopped onion, cilantro, lime or lemon juice, salt and pepper, and mash some more.
3. Add the jalapeños, starting with half of one and adding until you reach the desired level of heat. (Chiles vary individually in their hotness.)
4. Add the Anaheim chiles and gently stir.
5. Add the tomatoes, gently stir, and serve immediately.

Note: If not serving immediately, keep the tomatoes separate, cover with plastic wrap directly on the surface of the guacamole to prevent oxidation from the air. Refrigerate until serving.

mexican-style shrimp cocktail

This coastal beauty is served at nearly every port throughout Mexico. It's cool and refreshing, and if you want more heat, use spicy Clamato and add two tablespoons spicy horseradish.

Serves 5

Ingredients

2 pounds cooked shrimp
1 tablespoon crushed garlic
½ cup finely chopped red onion
¼ cup chopped cilantro
2 jalapeños, seeded and finely chopped
1 medium tomato, diced into ¼-inch pieces
½ cucumber, peeled, seeded, and diced into ½-inch pieces
1½ cups Clamato, or clam juice cocktail
¼ cup freshly squeezed lime juice
1 ripe avocado, chopped

Preparation

1. Place the shrimp in a large, non-reactive bowl. Add the garlic, onion, cilantro, jalapeño, tomato, and cucumber, and stir until combined.
2. Add the Clamato or clam juice cocktail and lime juice and stir gently.
3. Add the avocado and stir gently.
4. Spoon into martini glasses and chill until serving. Serve with lime wedges for garnish.

borracho scallops

Seared to perfection and drizzled with tequila and lime, these "drunken scallops" deliver all the enjoyment and flavor without the hangover.

Serves 4

Ingredients

$^2/_3$ cup fresh lime juice

¼ cup tequila

½ cup fresh lemon juice

½ cup sugar

2 jalapeños, and chopped seeded

1 cup chopped cilantro

1 tablespoon chopped garlic

½ teaspoon salt

1½ pounds large sea scallop, cleaned

1 tablespoon olive oil

3 teaspoon finely minced cilantro

1 lime, quartered

Preparation

1. Place all the ingredients, except the scallops, olive oil, cilantro, and quartered lime wedges into a blender or food processor and purée until completely blended. Transfer to a glass bowl and set aside.
2. Clean and pat dry the scallops.
3. Add the olive oil to a hot sauté pan and sear the scallops until they begin to caramelize (about 1 minute). Turn the scallops over and cook on the other side for about 1 minute more, being sure to not overcook. Cook for about 30 seconds more, add the blended mixture and bring to a boil.
4. Remove scallops and transfer to a covered dish and keep warm.
5. Continue to cook the sauce over high heat until reduced by half.
6. To serve, place the scallops on a plate, overlapping one another, and drizzle the sauce directly from the pan over them. Sprinkle with the cilantro and the juice from the lime wedges.

sweet potato gorditas

The trick with this dish is to work quickly after you've boiled the masa, mashing it with the sweet potato as soon as possible. These are great as an appetizer, but they may be served as an entrée. Also, make sure to buy sweet potatoes and not yams—they are not the same thing.
Serves 6

Ingredients
1 large sweet potato, peeled and cut into 1-inch cubes
2½ cups masa harina (meseca), reconstituted
1 cup plus 2 tablespoons water
1 tablespoon salt, or to taste
½ cup oil

Preparation

1. Boil the sweet potato until soft. Strain and then mash in small bowl and set aside.
2. Reconstitute the masa by mixing 2½ cups with 1 cup plus 2 tablespoons water.
3. Fill a large saucepan with about 2 inches of water, add the salt, and bring to a boil.
4. Meanwhile, line a large baking sheet with wax paper. Divide the masa into 4 equal parts and shape them into patties. Gently place each masa patty into the boiling water, cover and cook at a medium boil for 10 minutes.
5. Using a slotted spoon, gently remove the patties from the water and drain.
6. This is where you must work quickly! Add the cooked masa to the sweet potato and quickly mash the mixture together with a potato masher until well combined.
7. Transfer the mixture to a food processor and blend until the mixture has a smooth consistency, about 2 minutes.
8. Using your hands, form the mixture into 2-ounce balls (about the size of a ping pong ball; make approximately 15 balls). Place the balls on the prepared baking sheet and, using your fingers, flatten each ball into a 3½-inch wide circle, then form a lip around the edge of each circle, about ¼-inch high. Cover with a damp towel and set aside for up to 2 hours (any longer and they will dry out).
9. Heat the oil in a large saucepan over medium to high heat (375 degrees F). Place 4 or 5 shells into the hot oil, being sure that they do not touch. Cook on each side for approximately 1 minute (overcooking will make them soft). Remove and place on paper towels to drain.
10. Serve with toppings of your choice. Try this combination: a smear of pinto beans, 2 ounces freshly cooked chorizo or carnitas, a dollop of sour cream or avocado cream, crumbled Cotija cheese, and garnish of chopped red onion, chives, or cilantro.

These beauties (blue crab) were caught in three feet of water, twenty feet off shore in front of our house in Playa Miramar. Sweet blue crab meat makes the best enchiladas.

Entrées

Dinner is an event—a time spent with family and friends, a time to slow down, converse, relax, and reflect upon the day. Of course it's also a time to experience and enjoy great food. With life blazing by at mach speed, dinner has been nearly forgotten, overlooked, and to some it has even become a burden. In Mexico, this would never happen. The bond of family, friends, and loved ones is too great to be superseded by work, money, or things. There is much to be learned here.

A simple dinner with family and friends can restore much to our lives, creating cherished moments, making memories, laughing, and bonding.

With the recipes that follow it is my hope that you will allow life to stop and return to dinner. Refresh your spirit, become reacquainted with your loved ones, and never let cooking become a burden.

carnitas

It doesn't get any better than slow-roasted carnitas. This recipe differs slightly from what may be served in Old Mexico. Traditional carnitas is cooked in lard, pulled from the oil, chopped, and served directly in tacos and such.

This versatile dish is one of our most requested at Salsa Brava. It can be served in tacos, burritos, omelets, or just about anything else you can imagine. We use all natural pork—no hormones, no antibiotics. Our choice for cut of meat is the pork butt. (Not to be confused with the actual pig's butt.) The pork butt is actually a shoulder cut, and it can be purchased with bone in or out. The bone found in the butt is the clavicle, and any butcher can remove it, if preferred.
Serves 8

Ingredients

3 to 4 tablespoons Salsa Brava Season Salt (page 88)
4 pounds pork butt, cut into two-inch cubes, some
    but not all of the fat removed
1 cup water
1 teaspoon liquid smoke
1 medium onion, quartered
5 large garlic cloves

Preparation

1. Season the pork with the Season Salt.
2. Preheat the oven to 350 degrees F.
3. Place a roasting grate at the bottom of a roasting pan and then pour 1 cup of water in the bottom of the pan with liquid smoke. Place the pork on the grate and top with the onion and garlic. Cover.
4. Bake for 2 hours, remove the cover and bake for an additional hour or until the pork is fork tender.
5. When cooked through, shred the pork, retaining the juices and incorporating them into the meat. Serve with warm tortillas or use when making tacos, tamales, etc.

seeding & stuffing a poblano chile

The best way to seed this chile is to cut a 1- to 1½-inch slit, starting from the stem, down the side of the chile. Remove the seeds through this slit. Try to avoid running the chile under water to remove the seeds, as the vital and flavorful oils will be compromised. Use the same slit to stuff the chile. Be gentle during this process. Depending on the season during which the chile was grown, it will have thick, meaty walls or thin, delicate walls. Leave the stem attached.

poblanos chile Relleno

For as long as I can remember we've offered this as our Thursday and Friday special. We tried to change it one week so our customers could have something new. Big mistake. Our customers revolted. We got phone calls, e-mails, and letters in our suggestion box demanding that we bring it back. One customer wrote, "I will be forced to burn Salsa Brava to the ground if you do not return my rellenos." Another claimed, "My wife is so mad—for the sake of our date night please bring back the rellenos." Of course, these were all taken in good fun, and the special returned after a two-week vacation.

There are as many options for chile rellenos as there are for salsa. Some rellenos require a batter, and some require baking. This versatile food is limited only to your imagination. Relleno in Spanish is defined as a "stuffed food dish." So stuff away!
Serves 6

Ingredients

6 poblanos, roasted, peeled, seeded,
    and split open
¾ pound Jack cheese, thinly sliced
10 eggs, separated
½ cup flour

Pinch of salt
1 cup canola oil
Crumbled cotija cheese, optional

Preparation

1. Stuff each chile with approx 2½ ounces of cheese. Set aside.
2. Using an electric mixer, whip the egg whites at high speed until stiff peaks have formed.
3. Beat the egg yolks with one tablespoon flour and salt. Slowly mix the yolks into egg whites and stir until incorporated. Do not over whip as the batter will go flat.
4. Place the remaining flour on a plate and roll each stuffed chile through the flour, evenly coating them (this will allow the egg batter to grip the chili). Dust off excess flour.
5. Heat the oil in a large nonstick pan over medium heat.
6. Using a ladle or large spoon, place 2 ounces of the egg batter in the pan. Immediately place a chile seam-side down in the center of the batter and cover with 1 more ounce of batter. Cook on one side for 3 to 4 minutes, until browned. Gently turn the chile over and continue to cook for another 3 to 4 minutes.
7. Transfer to a plate covered with paper towels to remove the excess oil. Repeat this process until all the chiles are cooked.
8. Serve covered in Chile Relleno Sauce (page 36) or pour a pool of the sauce on a platter and place the chiles on top of the sauce and top with crumbled cotija cheese. Garnish with remaining cilantro from the sauce.

chile relleno sauce

Makes 2 cups

Ingredients

3 tablespoons olive oil (divided)
½ cup diced onion
3 cloves garlic, minced
3 large, ripe tomatoes, cored and roughly chopped
3 tablespoons minced fresh cilantro (divided)
2 bay leaves
1 teaspoon salt, or to taste
White pepper to taste

Preparation

1. Heat 1 tablespoon of the oil in a medium skillet and add the onion. Sauté over medium heat until onions are caramelized. Scrape the pan to remove the flavors left by carmelizing the onion.
2. Add the garlic and sauté for 30 seconds.
3. Transfer the onion/garlic mixture to the bowl of a food processor or blender and add the tomatoes. Purée until smooth.
4. Transfer the tomato mixture to the skillet, add the bay leaves and the remaining 2 tablespoons of oil. Bring to a simmer and cook for about 10 minutes or until the sauce is slightly thickened.
5. Season to taste with salt and pepper. Add 2 tablespoons of the cilantro and discard the bay leaves.

anaheim chile rellenos

Serves 8

Ingredients

8 Anaheim chiles, fire roasted, peeled, and kept whole (canned are fine)
1 pound Jack cheese
½ cup flour plus 3 tablespoons
12 eggs, separated
1 tablespoon water
¼ teaspoon salt
½ to 1 cup canola oil (or as needed for frying)

Preparation

1. Cut a slit in the side of each chile (take care to keep them in one piece). Remove the seeds and the membrane.
2. Cut the cheese into strips about 1 inch shorter than the chiles in length and ½ an inch in width and thickness. Place one piece of cheese inside of each chile and press the sides together gently to seal.
3. Place the ½ cup of flour in a shallow dish and dredge each chile, coating thoroughly. Place the chiles on a cookie sheet lined with wax paper and chill in the refrigerator for an hour.
4. Using an electric mixer, beat the egg whites until stiff.
5. In a separate bowl, combine the egg yolks, water, 3 tablespoons of flour, and the salt. Stir until smooth.
6. Gently fold the beaten egg whites into the egg yolk mixture.
7. Heat oil in a deep fryer to 375 degrees F. Dip each chile into the egg batter and then place on a saucer. Carefully slide the chiles off of the saucer into the fryer. Fry each chile for about 4 minutes per side, until they are puffed and golden in color.

carne adovada

(KAHR-nay ah-doh-VAH-dah)

Make no mistake…this is not for those with tender palates. The heat from the chile de arbol can be intense. Enough said! Decrease said heat by eliminating a portion of the chile de arbol.

Serves 8

Ingredients

2 cups packed chile de arbol, stems removed
4 tablespoons canola oil
4 to 5 tablespoons water
4 pounds pork loin, cut into ¼- to ½-inch pieces
2 tablespoons garlic salt
10 cloves garlic, chopped
1 tablespoon cumin
½ cup mild red chile powder
1½ tablespoons salt

Preparation

1. Place the chile de arbol, 2 tablespoons oil, and water in a blender and blend on high until it is completely incorporated and makes a paste. Add additional water by the teaspoon if needed.

2. Place the pork in a large, shallow bowl and pour the chile de arbol marinade on top. Add the remaining ingredients, cover, and marinate in the refrigerator for 2 to 4 hours or overnight.

3. Heat a heavy skillet over medium to high heat. Add the 2 remaining tablespoon of oil. Carefully add the pork and all of the marinade to the skillet. Cook for 5 to 7 minutes or until the internal temperature reaches 165 degrees F. Serve as an entrée or use as a filling for burritos and enchiladas.

chili colorado

Serves 8

Ingredients

10 dried New Mexico chiles, washed, stems and seeds removed
3 cups water
½ cup all-purpose flour
1 tablespoon kosher salt
1 tablespoon black pepper
5 pounds boneless beef chuck roast, trimmed of fat and cut into 1- to 2-inch pieces
3 tablespoons olive oil
1 large white onion, chopped
4 cloves garlic
2 cups beef broth or water

Preparation

1. Place the chiles and 3 cups of water in a medium stockpot and bring to a boil. Remove from the heat and steep for 30 minutes to soften.
2. Strain the softened chiles into a bowl, reserving the liquid.
3. Place the chiles and some of the liquid into a blender and purée until smooth. Add more liquid as necessary to form a smooth sauce.
4. Pass the sauce through a fine mesh strainer to remove any seeds and the tough skins; set aside.
5. In a medium bowl, combine flour, salt, and pepper. Dredge the beef pieces in the flour; set aside.
6. Heat the oil in a large pot over medium heat. Sauté the onion until tender and translucent, about 5 minutes. Add the garlic and cook for one minute more. Add the meat, a few pieces at a time so as to not overcrowd the pot, and cook until they are evenly browned.
7. Transfer the cooked meat to a plate and add more pieces to the pot to cook. When all the meat is cooked, return all the pieces to the pot. Add the chile sauce and stir.
8. Add the beef broth to just cover the meat. Bring to a boil over medium heat. Reduce the heat to low and simmer for 3 hours, or until the meat is tender. If necessary, adjust with more broth during cooking.

carne Asada

Carne Asada is a dish that literally means "roasted meat." It is one of the most popular varieties of food more commonly served in the northern parts of Mexico. It can be found as the main ingredient in tacos, tortas, burritos, and fajitas, or simply served alone as a meal. It is sold at Mexican meat markets called *carnicerias* in the Southwest. At Salsa Brava, we have tried many variations of the dish, using flank steak, skirt steak, flat irons, sirloin, and brisket. All work well, but we have found that skirt steak works the best.
Serves 4

Ingredients
2 pounds skirt steak

Marinade Ingredients
6 garlic cloves, minced
½ cup soy sauce
1 jalapeño, seeded and minced
1 teaspoon freshly ground cumin seed (lightly toast the seeds first)

1 large handful fresh cilantro, leaves and stems, finely chopped
1 tablespoon kosher salt and freshly ground black pepper
Juice of 2 limes
2 tablespoons red wine vinegar
½ teaspoon sugar
½ cup olive oil

Preparation
1. Lay the skirt steak in a large non-reactive bowl or baking dish. Combine marinade ingredients and pour the marinade over the steak, making sure each piece is well coated. Cover and refrigerate for 4 to 6 hours, or overnight.
2. Preheat an outdoor grill to hot or heat a cast-iron skillet if cooking indoors. Remove the steak from the marinade, season both sides with salt and pepper, and place it on the grill (if cooking indoors, remove excess marinade as the garlic may burn and smoke on the hot skillet).
3. Grill the steak for a few minutes only on each side, depending on the thickness, until it is cooked to your preference. You may need to work in batches.
4. When cooked, remove the steak to a cutting board to rest for five minutes. Thinly slice the steak across the grain on a diagonal and serve. (This recipe can easily be doubled.)

posole

[poh-SOH-leh]

This dish is really a thick, hearty soup that is usually eaten as a main course. It's most commonly made with pork but sometimes with chicken. The other main ingredients are broth, hominy, onion, garlic, dried chiles, and cilantro. Serve it with a medley of chopped lettuce, radishes, onions, cheese, and cilantro, which can be added to individual bowls as desired.

Posole originated in Jalisco, in the middle of Mexico's Pacific coast region, and it is traditionally served at Christmas. The real deal is made with oxtails and pig heads, and these are reserved for the matriarchs and patriarchs of the family. Traditional posole recipes can require most of a day to cook, but this version takes a little less time. Hominy is kernels of corn that have been soaked in lime water, hulled, and dried. *Serves 10*

Ingredients

3 tablespoons canola oil

3 pounds pork shoulder, cut into ¾-inch pieces

1 onion, chopped

4 cloves garlic, minced

10 cups chicken broth

1 teaspoon dried oregano

2 teaspoons salt

3 tablespoons ground mild red chile (New Mexico, Anaheim) or chili powder

4 cups canned white hominy, drained

Garnishes

Radishes, thinly sliced

Iceberg lettuce, shredded

Onion, finely chopped

Cilantro, chopped

Lime wedges

Preparation

1. Heat the oil in a large Dutch oven or heavy stockpot over medium-high heat. Add the pork and cook, turning, until browned on all sides, about 5 minutes. Remove the pork with a slotted spoon and transfer to a warming dish. Keep the rendered fat in the stockpot and reduce the heat to medium.
2. Add the onion and garlic to the pot, cooking just until the onion softens, about 3 minutes.
3. Return the pork to pot and add the broth, oregano, salt, and chiles or chili powder. Reduce the heat to low, cover, and cook for 90 minutes.
4. Add the hominy and cook for 15 minutes more. Adjust seasonings as necessary.
5. Serve with a variety of garnishes and hot corn tortillas.

Garnishes and toppings are an important component of great Mexican cooking. Radishes, fire-roasted chiles, cilantro and onion can be found at nearly all taquerias.

Flautas

Flautas is Spanish for flutes. Chicken flautas are traditionally served with rice and beans. You can also use carne machaca (Page 46), carnitas (Page 33), or adovada (Page 38) as fillings for flautas.
Serves 4

Ingredients
12 yellow corn tortillas
2 cups cooked, shredded chicken
Grated cheddar cheese
Cooking oil
½ Red Chile Sauce recipe (page 91), optional

Preparation

1. Heat a cast iron skillet or griddle to medium-hot. Place 2 tortillas on the hot surface for a few seconds, then turn and heat on the other side (this will make the tortilla pliable enough to roll tightly).

2. Transfer the heated tortillas to a work surface, overlap them, and place 1 heaping tablespoon of chicken and cheese along one side of the tortillas. Roll the tortillas into a flute as tightly as possible without tearing the tortillas. Weave two toothpicks into the overlapped tortillas to hold them closed. Lay the tortilla flute flap down on a plate, and continue filling and rolling the rest of the tortillas.

3. Heat about half of the cooking oil in the skillet over medium to high heat (about 375 degrees F). Carefully place the flautas, three at a time, flap side down in the hot oil and cook until they are golden and crisp.

4. Transfer the flautas to paper towels to drain the excess oil and keep warm until all the flautas are cooked.

5. Serve with garnishes of Avocado Cream (Page 93), Marinated Red Onion (Page 96), or sour cream and Guacamole (Page 23).

carne machaca

The great machaca debate! What is machaca? Many people swear by their tried and true recipes based on slow-cooking a beef chuck roast with different ingredients, shredding the carne (meat), and then serving. Others swear that machaca is really a variation of carne seca, which is essentially air-dried meat. I've had both versions, and both are very good. Of course they differ in flavor and texture. At Salsa Brava, we prefer the slow-cooked process rather than the air-dried, sun-dried, or oven-dried method. El Charro Mexican Restaurant of Tucson serves up a famous rendition of the air-dried variety, and patrons visit El Charro solely for this carne seca dish. Our machaca starts with a quality cut of boneless rump roast or chuck roast (be sure to use quality meat cuts; don't believe that because of the long cooking time a lesser quality of meat will do).
Serves 6

Ingredients

3–4 pound boneless rump or chuck roast, cut into
   4 or 5 equal-size pieces
2 tomatoes, diced
½ cup diced roasted green chile
1 cup beef broth
1 yellow onion, diced
10 garlic cloves, smashed

4 chipotles in adobo (use at least 2 tablespoons of
   the adobo sauce)
1 tablespoon ground cumin
1 tablespoon dried oregano
1 tablespoon kosher salt
½ tablespoon black pepper

Preparation

1. Preheat the oven to 350 degrees F.
2. Place the roast pieces on the bottom of a large, thick-walled stockpot. Add all of the remaining ingredients.
3. Cover the stockpot and place in the oven. Cook for 4 hours or until the meat pulls apart with little resistance.
4. Remove from the oven and transfer the meat to a cutting board. Reserving the liquid.
5. When the meat has cooled enough to handle, shred it using two forks. Moisten the meat with some of the liquid until it is moist but not dripping. Use the machaca in tacos, burritos, machaca con huevos, tostadas, etc.

Huevos Rancheros

In the sixteenth century the Spaniards arrived in Old Mexico. They brought chickens with them, and the huevo love affair began. Like many Latin American dishes, huevos rancheros blend old and new world culinary traditions. Huevos rancheros, or ranch-style eggs, were traditionally served at second breakfast—*almuerzo*—which took place around eleven o'clock in the morning.
Serves 4

Ingredients

2 tablespoons canola oil, or as much as is needed to fry tortillas
4 corn tortillas
2 chorizo sausages, cut into ¼-inch slices and browned
½ cup canned black beans, drained
Salt and freshly ground pepper, to taste
½ recipe Blackened Tomato Salsa, warmed (Page 2)

½ cup crumbled cotija or Jack cheese
8 eggs cooked as you like (scrambled, up, or over medium)
2 tablespoons sour cream
1 tablespoon coarsely chopped cilantro
1 avocado, cut into ½-inch cubes (optional)

Preparation

1. Preheat an oven to 350 degrees F.
2. Warm the oil in a large skillet over medium-high heat. Fry the tortillas one at a time, turning once, about 5 seconds per side. Using tongs, transfer tortillas to paper towels to drain.
3. In a small bowl, combine the chorizo and beans. Season with salt and pepper.
4. Place 2 tablespoons of the salsa on an oven-safe plate. Lay one tortilla on the salsa and top with one-quarter of the chorizo/bean mixture and two eggs. Place 1 tablespoon of the salsa and 1 tablespoon of the cheese on the eggs. Assemble all four of the plates and transfer them to the oven to cook for five minutes.
5. Remove from the oven and serve garnished with sour cream, cilantro, and avocado.

Maui Tacos

What started out as a mistake has turned into one of our bestsellers. One day we were blackening the pineapple for our Seared Pineapple Salsa, and as we pulled the roasting pineapple from the grill a small amount fell onto the flattop and got mixed in with an order of Carne Adovada. I threw it into a flour tortilla and the light bulb went off! These tacos are amazing and have even been shown on the Food Network.

Makes 10 tacos

Ingredients
½ recipe Carne Adovada (page 38)
½ cup chopped Maui sweet onion
1 cup diced fresh pineapple
2 tablespoons canola oil
Garnish—fresh chopped cilantro, cotija cheese and avacado cream (page 93)

Preparation
1. Heat a heavy skillet over medium to high heat. Add and heat the oil.
2. Add the Carne Adovada, the sweet onion, and the pineapple. Cook for 5 to 7 minutes or until the internal temperature reaches 165 degrees F and the onion and pineapple have caramelized.
3. Serve in warm, fajita-style flour tortillas. Garnish with fresh chopped cilantro, cotija cheese, and Avocado Cream (page 93).

tamales

Mexican tamales are packets of corn dough (masa) with a savory or sweet filling. They are typically wrapped in cornhusks or banana leaves, but other wrappings include avocado leaves or other nontoxic leaves, and even paper or bark.

The history of tamales dates back as far as 5000 BC, and tamales of old came in all shapes and sizes. There were meat, seafood, vegetable, nut, and fruit tamales. Some were filled with the corn dough masa we use today, and some were not. Crushed rice or beans could be used instead of the masa, or there was no masa used at all. Tamales were steamed, grilled, roasted, boiled, or even fried. Compared to what we are used to today, formerly there was quite a variety of tamales. Many variations of ingredients can be used in making tamales, such as a combination of beef, pork, chicken, roasted corn, or even fried beans. This recipe is a simple version of Salsa Brava's pork and red chile tamale. They can be labor intensive, but can also be fun for the whole family. Tamales freeze well, and our kids love to take them to school for lunch.

Makes 3 to 5 dozen

Ingredients

1 recipe Carnitas, plus all of the broth (Page 33)
1½ pints Red Chile Sauce (Page 91)
1 bundle hojas (cornhusks)
5 pounds fresh masa, or dried maseca prepared per package instructions
1½ cups canola oil or olive oil
1 tablespoons salt

Preparation

1. Combine the Carnitas (reserving the broth for later) with the Red Chile Sauce and set aside.
2. Soak the cornhusks in the sink or a large pot of warm water for about 2 hours or until they are soft. Separate them gently, being careful to not tear them.
3. Combine the masa, oil, salt, and enough broth to make a smooth paste. Using a mixer, mix until a small amount (1 teaspoon) floats in a cup of cool water.
4. Spread the masa ($\frac{1}{8}$- to ¼-inch thick layer, or to preference) on the cornhusks. Place a small amount of meat in the center of the masa and then roll up the cornhusks, folding up the ends.
5. Place the tamales, fold down, in a steamer with 1 to 2 inches of water. Cover with a tight-fitting lid and steam for about 30 minutes. (Tamale steamers can be found sometimes at specialty cooking stores.)

seafood ENTRÉES

More than six thousand miles of coastal bliss surround Mexico—some of the finest beaches and ocean life in the world! It's no wonder that seafood has played such an integral role in Mexican cooking.

On the Mexican coast, the early morning arrival of the panga boats signals a rush to the dock where business happens fast; at a rapid pace, money and seafood exchange hands and within minutes the fresh catch is cleaned and laid upon crushed ice as the sounds of men yelling out the day's fresh catch echo off the fishmarket's walls.

Wandering the sidewalks of Rocky Point's fishmarket is an enjoyable experience full of the sights and smells of fresh steamed clams, Mexican-style shrimp cocktail, carne asada, tacos al pastor, carne adovado, and fresh grilled shrimp and fish. The final finish to a great meal is an ice cold Pacifico while watching the pelicans dive with precision to catch their lunch.

This is where my love of seafood started and continues today.

seafood enchiladas with cilantro cream sauce

Serves 6

Ingredients

1 onion, chopped
1 tablespoon butter
½ pound fresh or (canned, drained) crabmeat
¼ pound shrimp, peeled, de-veined, and coarsely chopped
8 ounces pepper Jack cheese, shredded
8 ounces Cheddar cheese, shredded
12 (6-inch) corn tortillas
2 teaspoons chopped cilantro
1 recipe Cilantro Cream Sauce (Page 92)

Preparation

1. Preheat oven to 350 degrees F.
2. Add butter and onion to a large skillet and sauté over medium heat, until onions are transparent.
3. Add the crabmeat and shrimp and sauté for 2 minutes over high heat. Remove pan from heat.
4. Add half of the cheese to the pan and stir.
5. Dip each tortilla into the Cilantro Cream Sauce and place a large spoonful of the seafood mixture in the middle. Roll the tortillas up and place them seam-side down in a 9x13-inch baking dish.
6. When all of the enchiladas are prepared, spoon the remaining Cilantro Cream Sauce over them and sprinkle with the remaining cheese and garnish with chopped cilantro. Bake for 30 minutes.

chile relleno with tequila shrimp and cilantro cream sauce

Serves 4

Ingredients

2 tablespoons butter

2 cloves garlic, diced

¼ cup sweet canned corn, drained

1 cup chopped zucchini, (cut into ½-inch pieces)

¼ cup thinly sliced Maui sweet onion

¼ cup julienne red bell pepper

4 large poblano chiles, roasted, peeled, seeded, and sliced from the stem two-thirds down the chile

1 pound large shrimp (15 to 20 count) peeled, deveined, tail removed

2 ounces tequila

1 recipe Cilantro Cream Sauce (Page 92)

1 teaspoon cotija cheese

2 tablespoons chopped cilantro (1 for garnish)

Preparation

1. Melt the butter in a saucepan over medium to high heat; add garlic, corn, zucchini, onions, and bell peppers. Sauté for 3 to 5 minutes or until mixture begins to caramelize.
2. Add the shrimp and cook an additional 3 minutes.
3. At this point add the tequila to the pan. While the pan is still over the open flame, tilt it to ignite the tequila (make sure your face is well clear of the pan, as the tequila will flambé while the alcohol cooks off). Continue to cook for 2 to 3 minutes, but do not overcook the shrimp.
4. Remove from the heat and cool for 2 minutes.
5. Using a tablespoon, stuff each chili equally with the shrimp mixture.
6. To serve, place a large pool of the cream sauce on one side. Place the stuffed chiles in the center of the pool and top with more cream sauce, cheese and cilantro. Serve with rice and beens.

Tacos de Pescado (Fish Tacos)

In 1987, my best friend Charlie and I headed for the border for a six-week Mexican smorgasbord. We ended up in Zipolite just north of Puerto Angel on the Pacific coast. We had no sooner arrived in Charlie's old VW van when we were approached by a couple of kids with a string of pots thrown over their shoulders. They asked if we needed dinner. Given an immediate response of "yes," the boys were off to the surf and in a matter of moments had landed several fish. They started a fire on the beach, cleaned the fish, crushed the garlic, and made fresh corn tortillas warmed on the comel as the fish sizzled. Before we knew it, we were dining on the freshest fish tacos known to man…all for just two bucks!

How one cooks the fish for Tacos de Pescado is up to personal preference. It can be batter dipped or breaded and fried, or it can be grilled. Following is the Salsa Brava method for cooking fish or shrimp tacos. *Serves 6*

Ingredients

Beer batter (recipe follows)

2 pounds firm fish, halibut, cod, or red snapper (We use hoki, which is an Icelandic product with firm white meat)

½ cup flour

¾ cup canola oil

12 corn tortillas

¼ cup tartar sauce

½ cabbage, shredded

2 tomatoes, diced

1 avocado, diced

½ cup shredded cheese of your choice

Fish Taco Preparation

1. Prepare the batter and set aside. Place flour on a shallow bowl or plate and set aside.
2. Heat the oil in a heavy skillet to 375 degrees F.
3. Cut fish into 2- to 3-ounce fillets. Dredge the fillets with flour lightly, shaking off any excess flour.
4. Dip the fillets in the beer batter and carefully place them in the skillet. Cook until crisp and golden brown.
5. Steam the tortillas until they are warm (taking 4 tortillas at a time, completely submerge the tortillas in cool water and then place them on a non-stick hot griddle to steam for 30 seconds per side). Corn tortillas are my favorite for fish tacos, but feel free to use a small flour fajita tortilla, if preferred.
6. Serve the fish wrapped in the fresh-steamed tortillas and add a teaspoon of tartar sauce. Top with the shredded cabbage, tomatoes, avocado, and shredded cheese as desired.

Beer Batter

Makes about 2 cups

Ingredients

1 cup flour
2 teaspoons cornstarch
1 teaspoon baking powder
½ teaspoon salt, or to taste
1 egg
1 cup beer or ale

Batter Preparation

1. In a large bowl, mix the flour, cornstarch, baking powder, and salt together.
2. In a separate, small bowl, whisk the egg and beer together.
3. Quickly add the egg/beer mixture to the flour mixture. Mix well, but don't worry about a few lumps. (This batter can be used for fish, veggies, shrimp, or just about any other seafood.)

blackened salmon with mango salsa

Salmon, halibut, mahi mahi—this recipe works well with most firm fish. When shopping for fresh fish, always ask to smell it prior to purchasing. A fresh catch will not smell fishy, but it should have the odor of salty sea air. Don't be discouraged by fresh-frozen fish. The best salmon we have ever purchased was line-caught, wild salmon from the Copper River Delta in Alaska that was cleaned and IQF-ed (Individually Quick Frozen) on the boat deck five to ten minutes after it was caught. IQFed Copper River Delta salmon is dime bright and often will still have sea lice on the skin (that's a good thing); these clues ensure that the fish was processed immediately.

Serves 4

Ingredients

2 tablespoons olive oil
4 salmon fillets (6 to 8 ounces), fresh or line-caught IQF
1 recipe Salsa Brava Blackened Seasoning (Page 89)
1 tablespoon butter
1 recipe Mango Salsa (Page 17)

Preparation

1. Brush salmon fillets on both sides with olive oil and then dredge them through the seasoning.
2. In a large, heavy skillet over high heat melt the butter and add the fillets. Cook until blackened, about 2 to 5 minutes. Turn the fillets over and continue to cook until blackened and fish flakes easily with a fork. (Cooking times will vary per the thickness of the fillet. If using salmon, try cooking it to medium: the center will still be pink and semi-translucent and the fillet will continue to cook after it is removed from the heat. Medium is the ideal temperature; there's nothing worse than overcooked, dry salmon.)
3. Serve fillets topped with 2 ounces of the Mango Salsa on each.

roasted corn and green chile steamed clams

The most important step in preparing steamers is to feed them their last meal! Using a roasting pan, layer the clams and cover with cold water (if you're at the beach, use fresh, clean ocean water). Sprinkle corn meal over the clams and give them a turn so the water turns milky. Refrigerate for at least two hours. You'll see the clams begin to open and ingest the corn meal as, at the same time, they spit out any sand, thus leaving only beautiful, clean, sweet clams ready for steaming. After two hours or more, drain and wash the clams under cold running water.

Serves 5 to 10

Ingredients

2 tablespoons butter
1 cup canned sweet corn, drained
5 cloves garlic, chopped
1 small, yellow onion, diced
1 cup fire roasted mild green chile, diced
¼ pound butter, melted, for dipping
5 pounds live, little-neck or middle-neck steamer clams

Preparation

1. In a pot that is at least twice the size of the amount of clams to be cooked, over high heat, add the butter and the drained corn. Sauté for 3 to 5 minutes, until the corn begins to caramelize.

2. Add the garlic, onion, and green chile and sauté for 5 minutes.

3. Carefully add 2- to 3-inches of water to the pot, cover, and bring to a boil.

4. Add the clams, cover, and return to a boil, then adjust the heat to maintain a rapid simmer. Cook, covered, for 5 to 7 minutes, or until all the clams have opened (discard any clams that stay closed).

5. Serve the clams in large bowl with the stock poured over the top and with melted butter for dipping. Grab a fork, stab a steamer, dip in butter, and enjoy!

steamer clams

The FDA recommends soaking steamer clams for several hours in seawater (or in $1/3$ cup coarse kosher salt, 1 gallon of water, and 1 cup cornmeal). Use kosher or sea salt as the iodine in regular salt will kill the clams before they hit the boiling water.

One hour before serving, scrub the clams with a vegetable brush in cold water; rinse with water until the clams are free of sand (adding a little coarse kosher salt to the water will help to remove the sand from the clams).

soups

In Mexico, it's "soup of the day," and this first course is required on nearly every menu. Most Mexicans do not consider their meal to be complete without a bowl of soup to start it off. In nineteenth-century Mexico City, a typical start to the meal was a broth of chicken or beef with limes for squeezing and chile for garnishing.

This manner of serving broth with lime and chile has not changed, although *caldo de pollo*—chicken soup—is now commonly eaten in the morning, as is *caldo de mariscos*—seafood soup—which is also a classic hangover remedy. It is not unusual to see people in the small restaurants found inside the markets having these popular soups for breakfast.

Many cooks have their own favorite basic chicken and beef stock recipes, and serious vegetarians usually have their preferred recipes for vegetable stock. When making any of these recipes, try adding one or a combination of these firecracker tricks: to chicken, beef, or vegetarian stock, add one, two, three, or even a handful of chile de arbol to the stock, or add sprigs of cilantro.

Any of these soup recipes can be partnered with crusty bolillos, French bread, or warm tortillas, plus a salad.

classic tortilla soup

This soup is easy and quick to make, and it's flavorful and filling. Serve it with Pan de Elote (Page 83), or give it some smoky heat by adding a puréed chipotle. This soup freezes well.
Serves 4 to 6

Ingredients

1 (2½ to 3 pound) chicken, cut-up, skin removed
2 ribs celery, cut into chunks
1 medium onion, quartered
1 large carrot, quartered
2 sprigs parsley
2 tablespoons chicken soup base
1 teaspoons lemon-pepper seasoning
1 large clove garlic, minced, or granulated
   garlic to taste
1½ pounds potatoes, peeled
1 large can creamed corn

1 (10 ounce) can Rotel tomatoes, crushed
1½ cups half and half
2 to 4 tablespoons minced cilantro
1 cup shredded Cheddar cheese
1 cup shredded Jack cheese
1 cup sour cream
4 to 6 corn tortillas, cut into ¼-inch strips and deep
   fried until crisp
1 avocado, sliced
½ cup black olives, sliced

Preparation

1. Combine the first seven ingredients in a large stockpot and cover with water by about 2 inches. Bring to a rapid boil, lower the heat to a simmer, and cook for about 1 hour or until the chicken is tender and falling off the bone.
2. Strain through a sieve and retain the broth. Set the chicken aside to cool. Once cooled, shred the chicken into small pieces. Set aside.
3. Transfer 4 cups of the reserved chicken broth back to the stockpot. Place the potatoes in the pot and boil them until tender, about 20 minutes. Remove from the heat and add the creamed corn, tomatoes, half and half, and cilantro. Mash the potatoes (do not remove the broth) until all ingredients are thoroughly combined.
4. Return the pot to the stove and simmer on low for about 15 to 20 minutes. Taste and adjust the seasonings, adding salt to taste if necessary, while being careful to not add too much.
5. Just before serving, add the reserved chicken meat and cheeses. Cook until the chicken is heated through and the cheese has melted.
6. Serve with your choice of garnishes, such as sour cream, fried tortilla strips, avocado, and black olives.

Black Bean and chorizo soup

While well-made black bean soup is great as is, the addition of chorizo to this recipe adds some zip.
Serves 3 to 4

Ingredients

2 tablespoons olive oil
½ pound bulk chorizo sausage or 2 links Spanish
   chorizo, sliced
1 onion, chopped
1 clove garlic, crushed
½ green bell pepper, chopped
¼ teaspoon ground black pepper (optional)
½ teaspoon ground cumin

Salt to taste
4 cups chicken broth
2 cans black beans
½ cup cooking sherry
Garnishes:
Chopped onion
Chopped cilantro
Dollop of sour cream per serving

Preparation

1. In a heavy soup pot over medium heat, add the oil. Add the chorizo, onion, garlic, bell pepper, pepper, cumin, and salt. Cook until the vegetables are softened.
2. Add the broth and the beans and simmer, partially covered, for 15 to 20 minutes.
3. Lightly mash some of the beans to thicken the soup. Add the sherry and cook for another 5 minutes.
4. Serve with garnishes of chopped onion, cilantro, and sour cream.

albondigas soup

Serves 4

Ingredients

1 pound ground beef
¼ cup dry/seasoned breadcrumbs
2 tablespoons minced onion
2 tablespoons water
1 egg
½ teaspoon salt
2 teaspoons Tabasco
1 large green bell pepper, chopped
2 tablespoons vegetable oil
1 medium onion, chopped
1 garlic clove, minced
4 cups beef broth
1 can (16 ounces) crushed tomatoes, undrained
¼ teaspoon saffron threads, crumbled

Preparation

1. In medium bowl combine beef, breadcrumbs, onion, water, egg, salt and 1 teaspoon Tabasco. Mix well.
2. Shape into 1-inch meatballs. Cover and refrigerate.
3. In a large soup pot, heat the oil over medium-high heat. Add the green pepper, onion, and garlic. Cook until tender, about 3 minutes.
4. Add broth, tomatoes, saffron, and remaining teaspoon of Tabasco. Bring to a boil, reduce heat and simmer uncovered for 30 minutes, stirring occasionally.
5. Add the meatballs and simmer, covered, for 20 minutes or until the meatballs are cooked.

cilantro and carrots— one big happy family

Cilantro, or coriander, not only has two common names, but also two entirely different identities and uses. Cilantro—Coriandrum sativum— describes the first stage of the plant's life cycle and is the Spanish word for "coriander leaves." It is also sometimes called Chinese or Mexican parsley. After the plant flowers and develops seeds, it is referred to as coriander. Technically, coriander refers to the entire plant. It is a member of the carrot family.

When purchasing cilantro, look for leaves that are tender, aromatic, and very green. If there is no aroma, there will be no flavor. Fresh cilantro does not keep well, and the flavor of dried is not comparable. Unlike with parsley, feel free to use the stems as well, as they contain great flavor.

poblano and roasted garlic soup

This surprisingly mellow soup gives a hit of roasted chile and an elegant green color perfect for chile season.

Serves 4

Ingredients

2 tablespoons olive oil, divided
4 tablespoons butter
1 small white onion, peeled and roughly chopped
2 stalks celery, roughly chopped
2 medium carrots, peeled and roughly chopped
3 cloves roasted garlic
2 teaspoons cumin seeds, toasted and ground
2 teaspoons coriander seeds, toasted and ground
3 cups water or chicken broth
1 cup heavy cream
4 poblanos, roasted, peeled, seeds removed, coarsely chopped
Salt and freshly ground black pepper, to taste

Preparation

1. In a 4-quart saucepan, heat 1 tablespoon olive oil and the butter over medium high heat. Add the onion, celery, carrot, and garlic. Cook, stirring for 4 to 6 minutes, or until the vegetables begin to brown.
2. Add the cumin and coriander, and cook for 1 minute more.
3. Add the water or broth and the cream. Bring to boil and reduce heat to low.
4. Add the poblanos, salt and pepper and simmer for 45 minutes.
5. Purée the soup using either and immersion blender, or purée in batches in either a blender or food processor.
6. Serve with chopped cilantro for garnish.

spicy pumpkin soup with mexican cream and toasted pepitas

Perfect for those fall dinner parties—the beauty of this soup is that it can be prepared the day ahead. Sitting for a day gives the flavors a chance to blend.
Serves 10 to 12

Ingredients

½ cup whipping cream
½ cup sour cream
1 teaspoon fresh lime juice
6 tablespoons (3/4 stick) butter
6 cups finely chopped onion
3 cans (15 ounce) solid pack pumpkin
2 cups whole milk
1¼ teaspoons dried crushed red pepper
9 cups low-salt chicken broth
¾ cup shelled toasted pumpkin seeds (pepitas)

Preparation

1. Whisk the first 3 ingredients together in small bowl. Cover and chill for 2 hours. (This is the Mexican cream, and it can be made up to one week ahead.)
2. Melt butter in heavy large soup pot over medium heat. Add onions and sauté until translucent, about 10 minutes.
3. Add pumpkin, milk, and red pepper. Mix until well combined.
4. Working in batches, purée mixture in a food processor. Return to the pot and add broth. Simmer for 10 minutes to blend the flavors, stirring occasionally. Season with salt and pepper. (This can be made one day ahead. If making ahead, remove from the heat and cool completely. Cover and chill. When ready to serve, reheat, bringing to a simmer.)
5. Serve sprinkled with the pepitas.

Roasted corn and green chili corn chowder

In a perfect world, the soup would be started by firing up the coals on the grill, peeling back the husk from the corn, stripping out the silk, rubbing the corn with oil or butter (or drenching it with water), and twisting the husk back up. The corn would be placed on the grill and cooked, turning every couple of minutes, for 15 to 20 minutes. In an imperfect world, turn on the oven to 400 degrees F and proceed as above—except you don't have to turn the cobs.
Serves 6 to 8

Ingredients

8 ears fresh corn
2 tablespoons butter
1 onion, finely chopped
1 clove garlic, finely chopped
1 jalapeño, finely chopped
1 large potato, peeled and diced (the same size as corn kernels)

4 cups milk
2 cups cream
Salt, white pepper, and cayenne pepper to taste
Garnish:
Parsley, finely minced

Preparation

1. Roast the corn (as per instructions above) and then allow it to cool. Once cooled, cut the kernels off the cob and into a bowl, scraping hard at the end to get every bit of the "milk" out. This should yield 4 cups of corn.
2. In a large soup pot, heat the butter over medium heat and add the onion, garlic, and jalapeño. Cook until the onion begins to soften, 3 to 4 minutes. Add the corn and diced potato.
3. Add the milk and bring to a simmer. Cook slowly until the potato is tender, 15 to 20 minutes. Stir in the cream and season to taste with the salt, pepper, and cayenne.
4. Serve with minced parsley.

Lime

The citrus fruit most associated with Mexico is the lime. All over the country, limes are served with just about everything. They are squeezed onto fruit salads, all kinds of tacos, seafood cocktails, fish dishes, and roasted peanuts, as well as added liberally to many kinds of soups. They are served with beer, especially cans of Tecate—locals prep their cans of beer by slicing the lime in half, cleaning the rim of the can with it, and then squeezing and stuffing the other half into the can. Lime is also squeezed in large amounts right into a glass of beer to make the drink known as a *Michelada*. Cuba, the rum and coke drink, is served with the addition of lime, and the delicious *Limonada Preparada* is made with lots of fresh lime juice, sugar, and mineral water, making for one of the most refreshing combinations imaginable.

sides

Not all side dishes are created equally. Often restaurants will place limited importance on these ever-important accompaniments to the main entrée. At Salsa Brava, we pride ourselves in putting as much detail into the side dishes as we do our main entrées. The tantalizing side dishes are what tie the meals together. Imagine a mariachi band without the guitars or a symphony without the strings. Now imagine fresh roasted Carnitas without Frijoles El Charro or Chorizo and Eggs without the Pan de Elote. The side dishes are the cornerstones in a brick arch that hold the entire structure together.

salsa brava caprese with red chile vinaigrette

This is our twist on an Italian classic, and it will knock your socks off!
Serves 2 to 3

Ingredients

5 ounces fresh, high-quality mozzarella
   (in brine), sliced
2 large vine-ripened tomatoes, sliced
4 ounces organic spring lettuce mix
2 ounces jicama, cut julienne-style
3 ounces spiced pecans
½ cucumber sliced (cut on a bias)
1 recipe Red Chile Vinaigrette
Salt, to taste
Fresh ground black pepper, to taste
Crisp red and blue tortilla strips, optional

Preparation

1. Down one side of a large platter, arrange the sliced mozzarella and tomato, alternating the the two.
2. Place the lettuce next to the cheese and tomato and top with the jicama and pecans.
3. Place the cucumber slices next to the lettuce.
4. Generously drizzle the entire salad with the Red Chile Vinaigrette
5. Season with salt and pepper to taste.
6. Garnish with crisp red and blue tortilla strips.

red chile vinaigrette

Makes 3 cups

Ingredients

4 tablespoons balsamic vinegar
2 teaspoons black pepper
¾ cup honey
1 cup olive oil
2 tablespoons mild red chile powder
2 teaspoons garlic salt
1 cup apple cider vinegar

Preparation

In a medium glass bowl, combine all ingredients and whisk together until well combined. It will keep for up to two weeks in the refrigerator.

arroz verde
mexican green rice

The cilantro purée adds beautiful color and texture to this unusual rice dish. This is a highly requested dish for our vegetarian friends. For those who like it hot, add a fresh habanero during the puréeing stage.
Serves 4

Ingredients

2 poblanos, inner membrane and seeds removed
½ jalapeño, seeds removed
3 cloves garlic
1 cup packed fresh cilantro, divided
½ green (sweet) pepper, inner membrane and seeds removed
½ medium yellow onion
2 tablespoons canola oil
1 cup long-grain brown rice
2¼ cups vegetable broth (or chicken broth for non-vegetarian option)
¼ teaspoon salt, or to taste

Preparation

1. Combine chiles, garlic, half of the cilantro, green pepper, and onion in a blender or food processor. Pulse until finely chopped but not puréed. Set aside.
2. Add oil to a medium saucepan on medium-high heat. Add chile mixture and sauté for 3 minutes.
3. Add rice and sauté until grains are thoroughly coated, about 2 minutes.
4. Add broth and bring to a boil. Stir, reduce heat to low, and cover tightly. Simmer 40–45 minutes.
5. Remove pan from heat and let stand for 5 minutes. Fluff with a fork and add salt.
6. Garnish with remaining cilantro.

street-side marinated jalapeño chiles

I have yet to find a street-side taco stand in Puerto Penasco that doesn't offer these little devils as an accompaniment to fresh salsas. Pickled jalapeños are easy and will keep for months in the refrigerator. I think that they also make great gifts.

Makes 4 pints

Ingredients

4 tablespoons canola oil

2 pounds jalapeños

½ large white onion, thinly sliced

½ large red onion, thinly sliced

2 heads garlic, split in half vertically, outer peel (only) removed

2 large carrots, peeled and thinly sliced

3 cups distilled white vinegar

²/₃ cup water

3 heaping tablespoons dried Mexican oregano, crumbled

¼ cup firmly packed dark brown sugar

Salt and fresh cracked pepper

4 bay leaves

Preparation

1. In a large stockpot add the oil and cook the jalapeños, onion, garlic, and carrot over medium to high heat until tender, about 3 minutes.
2. Add the vinegar, water, oregano, brown sugar, bay leaves, salt, and pepper to taste and bring to a boil.
3. Remove from heat, cover with a tight-fitting lid, and cool completely.
4. Equally pack into 4 clean pint-size Mason jars. Top each jar with vinegar mixture and seal with Mason jar lid.
5. Bring 4 quarts of water to a boil and place Mason jar in the boiling water for 8 to 10 minutes. Remove from water and check for tight fitting lid.
6. Will keep for up to 2 months.

frijoles El charro

These beans are also known as caballero frijoles or Cowboy Beans. Using a Dutch oven over a crackling fire and a bed of hot coals to cook these—outside with the beautiful sun setting on the horizon over the Sea of Cortez—and they don't seem like work at all. Nothing's better then a lazy day of Dutch oven beach cooking. This dish can be served as a main course, especially if you don't want to leave the beach and the beautiful sunset. It is best served with a side of Navajo Fry Bread (page 81).
Serves 10-12

Ingredients

3 cups pinto beans (dried)

3 cups water

8 ounces bacon

$^2/_3$ cup diced onion

2 tablespoons chopped garlic

1 jalapeño, seeded and chopped

1½ tablespoons mild red chili powder

2 teaspoons ground cumin

1 tablespoon salt, or to taste

1 teaspoon white pepper

Preparation

1. Soak the beans overnight, being sure that they are covered entirely with water (3 cups should suffice).
2. Cook the bacon in the Dutch oven over a hot bed of coals until crisp, or if you're cooking in the kitchen, use a heavy stockpot with a cover.
3. Add the onions, garlic, and jalapeño and cook for 10 minutes.
4. Add the chili powder and cumin and cook for an additional 3 minutes.
5. Add half of the water from the soaking beans to the stockpot and scrape the bottom of the pot.
6. Add the beans and the remainder of the water. (If you're cooking beachside, remove a small amount of the hot coals to the side of the fire and place the oven on top of the coals.)
7. Cover and let cook for an additional 1½ to 2 hours (replace new coals after 1 hour).
8. When the beans are done cooking, add the salt and pepper. Keep warm until ready to serve.

navajo Fry Bread

My dad has a long history of collecting fine American Indian art, and as a result, I have gained a great appreciation and respect for Native American cultures. As a young boy, I would drive to Flagstaff with my family every summer to celebrate the Pow-Wow and visit the Museum of Northern Arizona. Fry bread was always on the menu. Half the fun was watching the families hand stretch the dough, fry it, and serve it directly to the waiting customers. Almost nothing compares to fresh, hot fry bread with sticky warm honey and powdered sugar.
Serves 8–10

Ingredients
5 cups all-purpose flour
1 tablespoon double-acting baking powder
1 teaspoon salt
$1^2/_3$ cups water
1 cup vegetable shortening

Preparation:
1. In a large mixing bowl whisk together the flour, baking powder, and salt.
2. Add the water, stirring until dough forms.
3. Transfer the dough to a floured surface and kneed until it forms a soft, but not sticky, dough. Transfer to a bowl, cover the bowl with a kitchen towel, and set aside for 1 hour to allow the glutens to break down.
4. Pull off egg-size pieces of the dough. Using a rolling pin, roll the pieces out on a clean, floured surface to about ¼-inch thickness and about 10-inches diameter. Poke a small hole (using your finger) through the center of each round so that they will fry evenly.
5. In a large skillet or Dutch oven, heat the shortening over moderately high heat until it is hot but not smoking.
6. Fry the rounds, one at a time, for 2 minutes on each side, or until they are golden. Transfer the fried bread to paper towels to drain.
7. Serve with powdered sugar and honey.

Green chile corn Bread (pan de Elote)

This is one of the most requested side dishes for the breakfasts we cater. If possible, when making this dish, fire roast fresh corn on the cob as well as fresh mild green chile. Pan de Elote is very forgiving. Feel free to experiment; add chopped chipotle, a blend of cheeses, pine nuts, or fire-roasted jalapeños.
Serves 8–10

Ingredients

1 cup yellow corn meal
1 cup all-purpose flour
1 cup sugar
1 tablespoon baking powder
½ teaspoon salt
¾ cup milk
2 eggs

6 tablespoons melted butter
1 small can diced green chile or 4 fire-roasted Anaheim chiles, peeled, seeded, and diced
1 small can baby yellow corn drained, or kernels from two fire-roasted whole corn cobs

Preparation

1. In a large, stainless or glass bowl, mix together the cornmeal, flour, sugar, baking powder, and salt. Mix until all ingredients are incorporated.
2. Add the milk and eggs. Mix with a wooden spoon or a hand mixer until there are no clumps.
3. Add the melted butter, chile, and corn.
4. Preheat the oven to 375 degrees F and bake for 20 minutes or until a knife inserted into bread comes out clean. For truly great presentation, bake in an 8-inch round iron skillet or a 9-inch by 9-inch baking dish. Grease the pan and preheat it in the oven for 5 minutes; this will ensure a nice firm crust on the bottom of the bread.

Flan

Serves 6

Ingredients

1¾ cups whipping cream

1 cup milk (not low-fat or nonfat)

Pinch of salt

½ vanilla bean, split lengthwise

1 cup sugar

$^1/_3$ cup water

3 large eggs

2 large yolks

7 tablespoons sugar

Preparation

1. Position oven rack in center of oven and preheat to 350 degrees F.
2. Combine cream, milk, and salt in a heavy, medium-size saucepan.
3. Scrape the seeds from the vanilla bean into the cream mixture and then add the bean itself.
4. Bring to a simmer over medium heat. Remove from heat and steep 30 minutes.
5. Meanwhile, in a separate heavy, medium-size saucepan, combine 1 cup sugar and $^1/_3$ cup water. Stir, over low heat, until sugar dissolves. Increase heat to high and cook without stirring until syrup turns a deep amber color.
6. Quickly pour the caramel into six ¾-cup ramekins or custard cups. Using oven mitts as an aid, immediately tilt each ramekin to coat the sides. Set the ramekins into a 13x9x2-inch baking pan.
7. Whisk eggs, egg yolks, and sugar in a medium bowl just until blended. Gradually and gently whisk the cream mixture into the egg mixture, avoiding creating much foam.
8. Pour custard through a small sieve into the prepared ramekins, dividing evenly (mixture will fill ramekins). Pour enough hot water into the baking pan to reach halfway up the sides of each ramekin.
9. Bake until the centers of each flan are gently set, about 40 minutes. Transfer flans to a rack and cool. Chill for about 2 hours before serving, or up to two days ahead of serving.
10. To serve, run a small sharp knife around the flan to loosen. Turn them over onto a plate, shaking gently to release the flan. Carefully lift off the ramekin allowing caramel syrup to run over the flan.

cotija cheese (the parmesan of mexico)

We use this fantastic, salty cheese for topping several of our dishes at Salsa Brava. Originally made from goat's milk, this cheese is strongly flavored, firm, and perfect for grating. It is used in Hispanic cooking similarly to the way Parmesan is used in Italian cooking. It is most often used to enhance the savory flavor of many dishes by mixing directly into recipes or sprinkling on top as a garnish.

condiments, seasonings, and marinades

salsa brava season salt

Makes ³/₄ cup

Ingredients
3 tablespoons sugar
4 tablespoons salt
1 teaspoon cracked black pepper
1 teaspoon turmeric
1 teaspoon onion powder
1 teaspoon garlic powder
½ teaspoon cornstarch

Preparation
1. Combine all ingredients in a small
   bowl and mix well. Store the prepared
   seasoning in an empty spice bottle or
   a jar.

salsa brava blackened seasoning

We use this to season chicken thighs, steaks, or fish
before searing on an iron skillet.
Makes ½ cup

Ingredients

1 tablespoon sweet paprika
1 tablespoon sugar
2½ teaspoons salt
1 teaspoon onion powder
1 teaspoon garlic powder
1 teaspoon cayenne pepper
¾ teaspoon white pepper
¾ teaspoon black pepper
½ teaspoon dried thyme
½ teaspoon dried oregano

Preparation

1. Combine all ingredients in a small bowl and mix
   well. Store the seasoning in an empty spice
   bottle or a jar.

sweet chile jelly

Don't be discouraged by the name of this jelly. The sweet sting complements our coconut prawns or roasted pork—and even bagels with cream cheese. At Christmas, we've been known to bottle our salsas for vendors and special guests. Last year we decided to bottle our sweet chile jelly. It is now the #1 requested Christmas gift.

Makes 2½ cups

Ingredients

1 cup chopped red bell peppers
½ cup chopped green bell peppers
⅓ cup chopped, seeded jalapeño
*½ habanero, seeded and chopped
   (use gloves when handling these little devils)
2¾ cup sugar

½ cup red wine vinegar
2 tablespoons fresh lime juice
6 tablespoons certo liquid pectin
* not ½ cup, only half of the habanero,
   otherwise the jelly will strip wax and
   remove paint

Preparation

1. Place the bell peppers, chiles, sugar, vinegar, and lime juice in a large sauce pan over medium heat. Cook until warmed and until the sugar has dissolved.
2. Transfer to a food processor or blender and pulse, being sure to not purée as there should be some texture to the jelly.
3. Return to the saucepan and bring to a boil. Mix well with a wooden spoon; do not let the mixture burn.
4. Skim the foam from the top and discard. Simmer for 5 minutes.
5. Add the pectin and continue to cook on high, until the pectin has dissolved and the mixture begins to boil.
6. Remove from the heat and cool.
7. While the jelly is still liquid enough to pour, transfer it to Mason jars. Don't cap the jars until the jelly has cooled. Refrigerate.

salsa brava red chile sauce

This classic red sauce is excellent because of its versatility. As you can see from the recipe, we never use red chile powder. We use sun-dried New Mexico chile pods from Arlos, a small family-owned farm. Their chiles are handpicked and sun-dried. The earthy flavor adds a kick to many of our dishes, such as our enchiladas, burritos, and huevos rancheros. For a vegetarian option, substitute the chicken stock with vegetable stock or water.

Makes 6 quarts

Ingredients
5 quarts chicken stock
8 cloves garlic, peeled and kept whole
1 pound white onions, quartered
8 ounces dried New Mexico chiles, stemmed and seeded
2 tablespoons canola oil
2 tablespoons all purpose flour
1 teaspoon salt, or to taste

Preparation
1. In a stockpot over high heat, bring the chicken stock, garlic, and onions to a boil. Simmer for 20 minutes.
2. Add the dried red chiles, making sure that the stock covers the chiles. Turn off the heat and steep for 15 minutes.
3. When cool, using tongs and a soup ladle, work in batches and place the chiles and stock into a blender and liquefy. (Be careful when blending hot or warm liquids, as the steam may build up pressure in the blender and explode out the top.) An alternative to this is to pour the stock through a fine mesh sieve, being sure to push the pulp of the chile through the sieve using the bottom of the ladle.
4. In a large saucepan heat the oil over medium heat and add the flour. Cook for 5 minutes, stirring often to create a roux.
5. Add the stock mixture to the roux and stir. Adjust the heat to low and simmer for 20 minutes and add the salt.
6. Cool and then transfer to an airtight container and store in the refrigerator for up to 3 days (it also freezes well). I use ice cube trays to freeze the sauce, and after they freeze, I pop them all out and store them in freezer bags, which allows me to use as much as I need at any time.

cilantro cream sauce

When the Food Network produced a segment for *Diners, Drive-Ins, and Dives* with Guy Fieri, he requested a handwritten version of this sauce.

Makes 1½ cups

Ingredients

2 tablespoons butter
1 teaspoon chopped garlic
2 tablespoon flour
¹⁄₃ cup heavy cream
¹⁄₃ cup milk
2 tablespoons chopped cilantro
½ teaspoon garlic salt
1 teaspoon salt

Preparation

1. Melt the butter in a saucepan, add garlic and sauté for 1 minute.
2. Add the flour and cook over medium heat, stirring constantly, to make a roux.
3. Add the cream and the milk and cook over low heat, whisking until all the ingredients are well blended, for about 5 minutes. Adjust the consistency as needed by adding one teaspoon of milk at a time. Add the cilantro, garlic salt, and salt and simmer over low heat for 5 to 7 minutes.

avocado cream

At Salsa Brava we prepare and use about five gallons of avocado cream every week. It's a simple and tart accompaniment to many of our dishes. Our Roasted Chicken Quesadilla, Maui Tacos, and Navajo Taco are all topped with this scrumptious condiment. It's best served out of a squeeze bottle for decorative purposes, but it's just as good as a dollop on top. The lime juice acts as a preservative for the fresh avocado and will prevent most of the discoloration that sometimes occurs with avocado.

To make Chipotle Cream, simply omit the avocado and substitute two chipotle chiles with one ounce adobo. Blend until creamy and smooth. Chipotle Cream will have a definite kick!
Makes 2 cups

Ingredients
1 cup sour cream
Juice of two limes
½ cup plain yogurt
2 ounces milk (use as needed to blend
    the cream into a fine purée)
1 avocado, pit and skin removed
Salt (to taste)
Garlic salt (to taste)
White pepper (to taste)

Preparation
1. Place all ingredients in a blender, cover and purée until smooth and free of any large avocado pieces.
2. Place in a squeeze bottle or a non-reactive glass bowl (if using a bowl place a piece of plastic wrap directly onto the cream). Refrigerate until using.

pollo asada marinade

This marinade works best with fresh, skinless, boneless chicken thighs.
Makes marinade for 10 thighs

Ingredients
¼ cup red wine vinegar
¼ cup soy sauce
¼ cup orange juice
½ cup 7-Up
1 teaspoon minced garlic
1 tablespoon mild red chili powder

Preparation
1. Combine all ingredients. When using to marinate
   chicken, marinate for 1 to 3 hours.

marinated red onion

These are available at nearly every taco stand in Mexico. They are a wonderful garnish for tacos de carne asada.

Makes about 1 cup

Ingredients

1 red onion
Juice of 2 limes
1 teaspoon kosher salt

Preparation

1. Cut onion in half width-wise, remove the skin, slice very thin (approximately $1/_8$ inch)
2. Place the onion slices in a shallow, plastic container.
3. Season the onion slices with lime juice and salt.
4. Mix until well incorporated.
5. Marinate for about three-quarters of an hour.
6. The onions will be a deep pink color when they are ready.

Drinks

The summer desert in Arizona burns hot and the cool mountain breeze chills the heart.

Start out the day with a taste of Mexico, or end the evening with one. Cool off on a hot summer day with our Salsa Brava Sangria or warm up on a chilly winter evening with our Mexican Hot Chocolate. Serve them at parties or curl up with your drink and a good book. Any one you decide to make is sure to please.

sangria

The beauty of the basic sangria recipe is that it is as delicious as it is easy, and it only gets better with time (as in 24 hours). You can spice it up with just your imagination. Really, it is hard to add the "wrong" ingredient here: think favorite fruits, spice, and liquors. Chill and enjoy!

classic red

Serves 4 to 6

Ingredients

1 bottle of red wine (Cabernet Sauvignon, Merlot, Rioja reds, red Zinfandel, Shiraz)

1½ lemons, sliced into wedges

1 orange, sliced into wedges

2 tablespoons sugar

1 shot brandy

2 cups ginger ale or club soda

Preparation:

1. Transfer the wine to a large pitcher. Squeeze the juice from the lemon and orange wedges into the wine. Once squeezed, add the wedges to the wine, leaving out the seeds if possible.
2. Add sugar and brandy, stirring well until sugar dissolves. Chill overnight.
3. Add ginger ale or club soda just before serving.

Note: If you'd like to serve it right away, use chilled red wine and serve over lots of ice. Addition ideas: sliced strawberries, peaches, a handful of fresh blueberries, raspberries, sliced kiwi, a shot or two of gin or rum, citrus soda pop, or lime juice.

classic white

Serves 4 to 6

Ingredients

1 bottle of white wine (Riesling, Albarino, Chablis, Gewurztraminer, Pinot Gris, Chardonnay, Sauvignon Blanc)

²/₃ cup white sugar

3 oranges, sliced into wedges (1 cup of orange juice may be substituted)

1 lemon, sliced into wedges

1 lime, sliced into wedges

1 shot brandy

1 shot rum

½ liter of ginger ale or club soda (ginger ale for those with a sweeter tooth)

Preparation

1. Transfer the wine to a large pitcher. Squeeze the juice from the fruit wedges into the wine. Once squeezed, add the wedges to the wine, leaving out the seeds if possible.
2. Add the sugar, rum, and brandy, stirring well until sugar dissolves. Chill overnight.
3. Add ginger ale or club soda just before serving.

Note: If you'd like to serve it right away, use chilled white wine, and serve over lots of ice.
Addition ideas: sliced strawberries, peaches, a handful of fresh blueberries or raspberries, or a cup of citrus-flavored soda pop.

margarita Etiquette

For the knuckleheads…
Of course, if you're an adult and drinking for flavor instead of for getting smashed, like the younger ones amongst us, you'll care more about overall taste, not alcohol strength.

For the knuckleheads, who wish to get wasted faster or more easily, follow this recipe:

Squeeze two or three limes, sweeten with a simple syrup made from Splenda, as it has been found to help your circulatory system absorb alcohol faster than real sugar does. Find the cheapest tequila you can. Tip your head back, open your mouth, and pour in the lime juice and tequila. Use a nifty funnel with a tube if you want to feel like a true party animal. Toss in a dash of margarita salt. Then find a pretty lampshade and put it on your head. The perfect picture of the party moron.

salsa brava top shelf margarita

Serves 1

Ingredients

2 cups granulated sugar

1 cup water

½ ounce Cointreau orange liqueur

½ ounce Grand Marnier orange liqueur

2½ ounces sweet and sour mix

1 ounce lime juice

1½ ounces 1800 Tequila

Preparation

1. First make the simple sugar by placing sugar and water in a small saucepan. Stir to combine and bring to a gentle boil over medium-high heat.

2. Reduce the heat and simmer until sugar is completely dissolved and syrup is slightly thickened, about 3 minutes. Remove from heat and let cool.

3. Transfer syrup to a container with a tight-fitting lid, cover, and refrigerate until ready to use. (This can be made weeks in advance and stored in a clean container in the refrigerator.)

4. Fill a shaker with ice. Add 1 ounce simple sugar and all the other ingredients. Shake well. Pour into a salt-rimmed glass and add a lime wedge or wheel.

oak creek blackberry margarita

A bounty of fresh blackberries emerges near the end of August and early September at the bottom of Oak Creek Canyon, near the confluence of the West Fork and Oak Creek. Our family has made this an annual berry-picking pilgrimage. If you make the trip, be sure to wear long-sleeve shirts, long pants, gloves, and closed-toe shoes. Fresh Oak Creek blackberries make the best margaritas.
Serves 2

Ingredients
4 ounces fresh-picked Oak Creek blackberries,
   or store bought
1 teaspoon sugar
4 ounces Cuervo Gold tequila
1 ounce orange liqueur
2½ ounces lime juice
2 cups crushed ice

Preparation
1. Blend berries in blender for 10 to 12 seconds.
2. Add the remaining ingredients and blend until ice is almost smooth.
3. Serve immediately in 12-ounce glasses.

Hit-n-Run "Grande" Margarita Mix

When you're tired of making just one margarita at a time, here's a recipe that'll make you about 35 (10-ounce) margaritas in one pop. Call a cab!
Serves 35

Ingredients

1½ quarts simple syrup
3 quarts lime juice
3 quarts, +1½ cups Cointreau
4 quarts plus ½ cup tequila

Preparation

1. Prepare the simple syrup first by bringing 6 cups of water to boil in a large saucepan. Add 2 cups of sugar, bring to a boil again, and stir until the sugar has completely dissolved. Remove from heat and cool completely.
2. Pour the simple syrup and all of the remaining ingredients into a large pitcher, mix well, and taste. Adjust the flavor as necessary with more simple syrup or lime juice.
3. Serve immediately to a large group, or pour the margarita mix into smaller containers and freeze for later use.

cabo waborita

This is a story about Sammy Hagar, Van Halen, and tequila. Sammy Hagar created this awesome tequila in 1996 while in Guadalajara, Jalisco, and brought it back to serve at his nightclub, Cabo Wabo, in Cabo San Lucas, Baja California Sur, Mexico. It's the genuine article—100 percent weber blue agave, baked in wood-fired adobe ovens and double-pot distilled the old-fashioned way for a rich, soul-warming taste. This is one of my favorite boutique tequilas—not cheap but the real deal.
Serves 2

Ingredients

2½ ounces fresh lime juice
2½ ounces triple sec
4 ounces Sammy Hagars Cabo Wabo tequila

Preparation

1. Fill a shaker with ice. Add all the ingredients and mix well.
2. Serve in a salt-rimmed glass.

mango margarita

The mango is the most widely consumed fresh fruit in the world, with worldwide production exceeding 17 million metric tons a year. Mexico is the largest exporter of mangoes in the world.
Serves 1

Ingredients

1½ ounces silver tequila

1 ounce triple sec

1½ ounces freshly squeezed lemon juice

2 ounces simple syrup (Page 101) or sweet-and-
   sour mix

¾ cup partially frozen, fresh mango pieces

Preparation

1. Place all ingredients into a blender and blend
   until completely combined.
2. Taste and adjust the flavor by adding more
   simple syrup or tequila.

Havana Mojito

The mojito was born in Havana, Cuba. There are many variations of the drink. This recipe calls for the five customary ingredients of mint, rum, powdered sugar, lime, and club soda. The story of the mojito is the story of pirates, plunder, and the pursuit of treasure. English corsair, Sir Francis Drake, on his quest for the fountain of youth, was encouraged to sack and plunder Spanish cities in the new world for Queen Elizabeth I. One of Francis Drake's subordinates, Richard Drake, came up with a cocktail that he spread to all of the sacked cities throughout the Caribbean. His cocktail, the Draque (meaning "the dragon"), is the precursor to the mojito. This was thought to be a medicinal drink that helped pirates fight off scurvy. Locals would consume it as a cure to many ailments and diseases that were so common at the time. The Draque evolved into the mojito when the founder of Bacardi rum substituted the original liquor with light rum.
Serves 1

Ingredients
5 mint leaves
Juice of 1 lime
1 teaspoon powdered sugar
2½ ounces white rum
2 ounces club soda
1 sprig of mint (for garnishing)
Crushed ice

Preparation
1. Place the mint leaves in a 16-ounce shaker and pour the lime juice over them.
2. Add the powdered sugar and then muddle the mint, lime juice, and sugar together.
3. Add crushed ice.
4. Add the rum, stir, and top off with the club soda.
5. Pour into a glass and garnish with mint.

mexican calienta chocolate

Christmas in the Conley family is spent south of the border at the edge of the Sea of Cortez at our home on Playa Miramar. Presents are wrapped and tucked neatly under the tree. Ole Saint Nick is always in for a treat when he slides down the chimney—Sage's homemade Christmas cookies and Mexican hot chocolate. Saint Nick always leaves with a smile. This is far and beyond the best hot chocolate ever. *Serves 2*

Ingredients
4 ounces Ibarra Mexican chocolate
2½ cups milk
Whipped cream (optional)
Canela sticks (Mexican cinnamon) for garnish

Preparation
1. Chop the chocolate and transfer to a blender.
2. In a small, heavy pot, bring the milk to a boil. Immediately pour the hot milk into the blender and blend until the chocolate is thoroughly incorporated and the mixture is frothy.
3. Serve topped with whipped cream and garnish with a canela stick.

Horchata (Arroz Agua)

Serves 3 to 4

Ingredients

1 cup uncooked white long-grain rice
5 cups water
½ cup milk
½ tablespoon vanilla extract
½ tablespoon ground cinnamon
²/₃ cup sugar

Preparation

1. Pour the rice and water into the bowl of a blender; blend until the rice just begins to break up, about 1 minute. Let rice and water stand at room temperature for a minimum of 3 hours.
2. Pour the rice water through a strainer into a pitcher and discard the strained rice.
3. Stir the milk, vanilla, cinnamon, and sugar into the rice water. Chill and stir before serving over ice.

acknowledgments

I love Mexico—its people, traditions, food, and culture. Mexico and all that it has to offer has given me countless gifts: a place to relax, decompress and experience true family bliss, and a better understanding and appreciation of family and its importance. Mexico encompasses a culinary world as creative and inventive as any that the Earth has to offer.

And so I acknowledge and embrace all that is Mexico. To the cooks and chefs who together have had so much creative influence on my life and the inspiration behind the food that I create. The farmers, fishermen, and ranch hands whose sweat and callused hands have provided the ingredients with which to cook, thank you. And I am forever appreciative of the core family values that are so cherished by all of these extraordinary people. I thank you.

To our loyal customers, it's been a pleasure cooking for you; and to the hundreds of employees who have passed through the doors of Salsa Brava over the past twenty years, each and every one of you has graced the restaurant and imparted a little slice of your knowledge, love, energy, and expertise. Salsa Brava is what it is today as result of all who have passed through these doors. To Brandon, our general manager, and the current staff, for allowing me to dedicate the time and energy to this book— muchas gracias!

To Rudy Ramos, art director/graphics and designer extraordinaire, whose calmness and creativity so diligently pushed this project forward.

A writer I am not, so special thanks to Claudine Randazzo, our editor, for interpreting all of my chicken scratch and countless e-mails and constructing them into a tangible body of work.

Chris Marchetti, our faithful photographer, here's to sitting around the campfire, telling lies, listening to the waves crash on the beach, and sprinting across the sand to get that last shot as the sun set. Your endurance and compassion are contagious (peace and strength); your photos are amazing!

Charlie Cambell—who, as a young man, was my guardian angel—for telling me how it is. Regina Dehr, for taking a big chance on a very young man twenty-some years ago.

Robert Reed, my office manager, the glue, duct tape, and sticky pads that hold my business life together. Arismundo Hernandez, my faithful sidekick in the kitchen, thank you for fifteen years of consistent, hard work. And to all our cooks past & present.

Special thanks to Anne Minard for that extra set of eyes.

George and the crew at Flagstaff Farmers Market, thanks for watching out for me and our customers. Charlie Horton and Roger Pisacanno, your wisdom, living example, and countless sweat lodges have truly changed my life.

Mark Lambertson, from Mountain Sports, for showing us all how to downsize with style. Executive Chef Frank Branham from The Cottage Place, for your camaraderie and willingness to share your expertise with so many in our industry and with the young, future chefs you inspire at our local high schools. It's been a pleasure to work side by side with you.

Paul Brinkman, my lawyer, who still threatens me when I've signed a document without his approval. Gabe, our plumber—you have no idea how important you are to us.

Wanda and Howard Whelcher for the foundation.

To Guy Fieri, the Food Network and Page Productions for putting us on the map!

My mom, dad, and siblings (Dory, you are forever in my thoughts; Mary Pat; Cathy; Jim; Peggy; and Mary Beth) for all of your encouragement.

And finally, my wife Genevieve—your love, compassion, encouragement, and patience have forever changed my life. And my daughter Sage, who has taught me to slow down in the kitchen—thanks, I needed that! My son Adam, your gifts are unlimited, and Ivan for keeping me young at heart.

index

about the author

John Conley was born in Phoenix, Arizona, where he got his start in cooking at a young age. With this love of food and cooking embedded early on in life, and the inspiration to open his own restaurant, John attended Northern Arizona University's renowned School of Hotel and Restaurant Management. He chased his dream and opened his first restaurant, Salsa Brava, at the age of twenty-one. It was here that he met Genevieve, his wife of sixteen years.

John was awarded "Chef of the Year" by his peers from the Northern Arizona Chapter of the American Culinary Federation in 2005 and honored with the President's Award in 2006 for outstanding culinary skills and community involvement. The readers of the *Arizona Daily Sun* have voted Salsa Brava the best Mexican restaurant four times and best salsa eight times.

He loves spending as much time as possible at his home south of the border cooking on the beach, or at his cabin in the wilds of Alaska. He and Genevieve have three children, Sage, Adam, and Ivan.